Sant Kirpal Singh Ji
(1894-1974)

KIRPAL SINGH

GODMAN

No man knoweth the Son, but the Father; neither knoweth any man the Father save the Son, and he to whomsoever the Son will reveal him.

MATTHEW 11:27

SAWAN KIRPAL PUBLICATIONS

Library of Congress Catalog: 78-68503
ISBN 0-918224-07-1

First published by Ruhani Satsang, Delhi, 1967
Second Edition, 1971
   Second Printing, 1972
   Third Printing, 1974
This Edition published by Sawan Kirpal Publications, 1979
Bowling Green, Virginia
Printed in the United States of America

*Dedicated
to the Almighty God
working through all Masters who have come
and Baba Sawan Singh Ji Maharaj
at whose lotus feet
the author imbibed sweet elixir of
Holy Naam—the Word*

Preface to the Third Edition

Sant Kirpal Singh, the author of this book, announced in 1974 the dawn of a Golden Age of Spirituality. The growing interest in Eastern philosophy, in life after death accounts, and in out-of-body experiences, points to an unmistakable shift in man's quest for happiness and fulfillment from the outer world to the self within.

There is no substitute for a living teacher. Even in respect of secular knowledge, where we have a vast body of published literature, we send our young to study under professors at school and college. How much more important to have a living teacher in the domain of spiritual knowledge which involves a dimension where our parents and friends can hardly help us.

Accordingly, in the mystic tradition, the role of the Guru or Master has been always regarded as primary. The discovery of such a competent guide who has himself realized God is, for the spiritual seeker, more than half the battle won. At the theoretical level, he alone can help us to a right understanding of the scriptures for he has himself experienced the truths they embody. At the practical level, he can charge us with his living impulse and enable us to transcend body-consciousness. Once up, he guides us in his radiant spirit-form through the inner planes of creation until we unite with our Creator and attain life's supreme goal. It is then that we realize that the perfect Master, though a man like us, is one with God—in short, that he is a *Godman*. He alone can offer the sincere seeker a way up and a way out. He holds the key to the mystery of life and death.

In this age of commercialism, the spiritual renaissance we are witnessing has not been lost on the advertising expert and the public relations specialist. The widespread involvement of the young in particular has left the door wide open for exploitation by charlatans, promoters and even by self-deluded fanatics. In cashing in on this new market, no gimmicks, no gadgets, are left untried, and the unsuspecting are held out the promise of an easy, almost instant, nirvana. In the mad array of sadhus, yogis, gurus and mahatmas who have mushroomed up within the past decade, how is the seeker to recognize a true Master, a real Godman? One mistake—and the opportunity of a lifetime may be lost! We have lately seen too much of the fanaticism, the cultism and the tragedy that ensue when we lack a proper norm and rely only on our own good intentions when making such a choice.

What makes Sant Kirpal Singh's book so basic and so indispensable is the infallible yardstick it provides to the spiritual seeker for recognizing a Godman. Here we have for the first time a clear and comprehensive guidebook for finding a spiritual Master of the highest order. Taking a step-by-step approach, the author explains who a Master is, what he does, the many grades of Mastership, and how one may distinguish a perfect living Master. Even beyond this, he explains to the reader how to make the quickest inner progress once he has found such a guide.

Just as we cannot know God unless He reaches down to us and enables us to share in His Consciousness, so we cannot hope to know and understand the Godman unless such a one reveals himself to us. Sant Kirpal Singh was such a realized soul and that is why his book is so valuable. He speaks with the clarity and conviction possible only to those who have direct firsthand experience. And he has the completeness of perspective which is possible only to a Master of the highest attainment.

Wherever he went during his lifetime, Sant Kirpal Singh brought a new conviction of the reality of God and of His Love and Fatherhood. Thousands around the globe experienced the living spiritual impulse he gave at the time of initiation into the Mysteries of the Beyond. He gave this freely, without charge, and many of his disciples testify to the manner in which he continues to guide them within, even after physically passing from among them in 1974. The individual saint may die, but Mastership carries on. He himself used to say that one bulb fuses and another is put in its place. Likewise, the principle of Mastership continues unbroken. And so, though Sant Kirpal Singh is no more among us physically, his spiritual mission continues, being carried on by Sant Darshan Singh who has his headquarters at Kirpal Ashram in Vijay Nagar, Delhi.

Vinod Sena, Ph.D.
Department of English
Delhi University

Introduction

According to some religious traditions we are living in the *Kali Yuga*—the final age of development on earth. People of all sorts and needs are entering society to make the final attempts toward Divine Realization. Central to these efforts to expand consciousness naturally is the Guru.

The Guru is much more than teacher in our sense, rather he is "The Spiritual Father." This enlightened presentation of the Guru should clear up many questions which have arisen in the minds of those who have their feet on the Path.

One vital point for the religious seeker today is the need for a Guru. One might say that the "Inner Guru" is the ultimate refuge; why bother to search in that jungle outside for a Living Guru?

True, the Inner Guru is the ultimate refuge; but in our age we all too often find the inner world a confusing labyrinth while the external world is our familiar playground. It is for this reason, to provide pathways through this labyrinth, that this book is so vitally necessary for our time. We are here told how to find our way among the welter of teachers and sects to find the True Guru, the *Sant Satguru*— the Inner Light and Word.

Even for the intellectually oriented western mind, these discourses on the Guru enlighten us on one major mystery which the Christian Church finds insoluble. That is, how can the incarnation be both God and man? This problem is solved here and in a most universal way, clear and timely for our age, yet as an answer very ancient to India.

The universality of this message cannot help but be a benefit to our age and be the groundwork for a much needed universality in religion. I would certainly commend this to every seeker.

WILLIAM BEIDLER, PH.D.
Department of Philosophy
Queens College
Charlotte, North Carolina

Hazur Baba Sawan Singh Ji
(1858-1948)

Author's Preface

For twenty-four short, beautiful, inspiring years, it was my blessing to be under the love, guidance, and protection of a Godman, Supreme Master Hazur Baba Sawan Singh Ji Maharaj.

Introducing the zealous seeker after Truth to a Godman is answering the perennial queries:

What is God?
How can His creation know Him?

It is my privilege to relate the mission of a Godman: Commissioned from above to give free to suffering humanity the gift of *Naam* (*Shabd*) the effulgent melody—the symphonic radiance which leads the *jiva* (embodied soul) back to his Father's Home.

If only the *atman* (soul) could be contacted with the Shabd this "string from the Nameless Lord" would lead to His door. But the spiritual faculties are so fogged and cloaked with gross coverings of mind and *maya* (illusion), that even though Shabd is reverberating within and around, the Soul cannot hear Its music nor see Its glory. How can man once again revive his link with his Maker?

Dhur Khasme Ka Hukam Paya;
Bin Satguru Chaitya Na Jai.

(Such is the Will of the Lord; He cannot be known except through a living Satguru.)
                                     VAR BIHAGRA 556

Without the enlivening touch from the living Satguru, the soul cannot awaken from Its slumber and get attuned to Naam.

We are familiar with:

*In the beginning was the Word . . .
And the Word was God.*

And:

Word was made flesh and dwelt among us.

So, Godman is the Word, the *Logos,* the *Naam (Shabd),* the *Kalma,* the *Akash-Bani,* the *Sraosha,* and the *Udgit* of the various religions of the world.

To the lovers of the Scriptures, the explanation is given of scriptural limitations.

To those who adore past Saints, historical evidence is given on their just immortality.

It is impossible to reduce to bare statement a Godman's words of wisdom, of peace, of consolation, of reassurance, of encouragement, of loving reprimand, which he utters as he moves among his disciples. His acts of selfless kindness and superhuman love bring home to those around him the unquestioning conviction of the Truth that he teaches.

But his life, conduct, influence, and blessings are indelibly recorded on those who earned this gift of Association.

His controlling power and solicitude inspire the jiva to surrender at his feet to be forever guided by his Word.

May the indefatigable seeker after the Mystery of Life find eternal rest in his Naam.

KIRPAL SINGH

Living Master
Sant Darshan Singh Ji

TABLE OF CONTENTS

Preface to the Third Edition vi
Introduction x
Author's Preface xiii
  1. Guru: What He Is 1
  2. Guru is Shabd 7
  3. Gradations in Mastership 18
  4. Guru: One or Many 23
  5. Present Master 26
  6. The Need of a Master 31
  7. Past Saints 35
  8. Without a Guru All is Darkness 59
  9. Historical Evidence 62
10. Before and After Guru Nanak 65
11. Scriptures and Their Value 68
12. Guru is Superman or Godman 75
13. Master and the Homegoing of Jivas 82
14. Master and His Mission 85
15. Master and His Work 88
16. Master and His Duties 90
17. Guru is Godman 93
18. Gurudev 100
19. Perfect Master 110
20. How to Find a Perfect Master and Know Him ... 112
21. His Life and Conduct 115
22. The Physical Form of the Master 117

23. The Influence of the Master 118
24. Oneness of Guru, Gurudev, Satguru & Malik ...133
25. The Nature of Oneness 136
26. The Blessings of God and the Master 151
27. The Solicitude of the Master 159
28. Master and the Controlling Power 169
29. Surrender to the Master 171
30. The Words of the Master 178

Thou art the pilgrim's Path, the blind man's Eye,
The dead man's Life; on Thee my hopes rely;
If Thou remove, I err, I grope, I die.

Disclose Thy sunbeams, close Thy wings, and stay;
See, see how I am blind, and dead, and stray;
Oh, Thou, that art my Light, my Life, my Way.

FRANCIS QUARLES

Godman

CHAPTER ONE

Guru: What He Is

> 'Tis much that man was made like God, before,
> But, that God should be made like man, much
>   more. . . .
>
> God clothed Himself in vile man's flesh, that so
> He might be weak enough to suffer woe.
>
> JOHN DONNE

IT IS well nigh impossible to know the Master and to understand his greatness. We have not the eyes wherewith we may behold his Reality. A prophet alone can know a prophet. We, the embodied spirits living on the plane of the senses, simply cannot know him.

> What Thou art we know not;
> What is most like Thee?

Again:

> How can the lesser the Greater comprehend?
>   Or finite reason reach Infinity,
> For what should fathom God were more than
>   He.
>
> DRYDEN

In *Jap Ji* (the daily morning prayer of the Sikhs), it is mentioned:

Unless one rises to His level, one cannot know of Him (God).

A Master Soul may be likened to a skylark, which is described as:

Ethereal Minstrel! Pilgrim of the Sky.

He who can soar as high as the skylark and follow her course may know something of the ethereal pilgrim; but poor crows and doves cannot. The Master is, however, not a pilgrim of the sky, but a denizen of the highest Spiritual Realm, and he comes down to sing to us the "Ethereal Song," and to take us along with him to his heavenly abode. While on earth, he is:

Type of the wise, who soar, but never roam;
True to the kindred points of Heaven and Home.

He is far beyond the limitations of the three bodies (physical, astral, and causal); of the three innate, natural and native propensities or instincts (*Satva, Rajas,* and *Tamas;* i.e., of righteous actions, worldly actions, and inertia or inaction, or actions born of ignorance and darkness); of the five elements of which the entire creation is made (earth, water, fire, air, and ether); and of the twenty-five *Prakritis* (i.e., subtle forms of varying degrees of which the elements are compounded); and also of mind and matter.

Shamas-i-Tabrez therefore describes him as:

He is a lark that lays a golden egg;

that is, an egg that shines like solid gold; the reference being to the Light of *Naam* or Word that is bestowed on each individual at the time of his Initiation.

He rides the high heavens every morning.
When he races, he covers all the solar systems,
And when he goes to bed, he makes pillows of
the Sun and the Moon.

In other words, when he is not engaged in any worldly pursuits he crosses over into higher regions for rest.

O Shamas-i-Tabrez! by just one kindly look,
He can give sight to thousands of stark blind
(i.e., make them seers and prophets).

Such Master Souls are in fact one with God, but come down into the material world at His behest to fulfill His divine purpose. Out of compassion for the world-weary souls, thirsty and hungry, moaning for reunion with the Beloved, God has to make provision for their homecoming.

As man alone can be a teacher of man, God has to send forth His Elect with a direct commission to lead back those who will listen to God's Message. He works as a means to an end.

Standing on the top of a hill, as it were, he can locate the smoldering fires of love in the various human hearts, and like a great and powerful magnet or lodestar, he draws all such individual souls as come into his sphere of influence, and by personal instruction and guidance works out the Divine Mission.

Each soul gains in spiritual grace in proportion to her receptivity. The more a person develops this receptivity, the more he experiences grace and spiritual benefit. Gifted with a limitless spiritual wealth he generously bestows it on all who aspire for it. Each gets according to his need and capability, and gradually develops the seed sown in him.

Sheikh Mueen-ud-din Chishti says:

*They (Master Souls) live in the world, but
their spirit is ever in the High Heavens;
Imprisoned in the tentacles of the body, their
spirit soars high above.*

Maulana Rumi also says:

*Never take a Godman at a human level; for he
is much more than he seems.*

Apparently, and in generalities, all men look alike, though each differs from the other in inner development. It is this background that helps each individual on the spiritual path and determines the measure of every step he takes, and, consequently, each one has his own time factor.

A Master Soul in human form cannot be rightly comprehended. He is a limitless ocean of *Sat* or Truth— ever the same from the beginning of creation and from age to age. As it is not possible to do justice to God's greatness, so we cannot do justice to God's elect.

A Persian Saint tells us:

> *He is beyond comprehension, apprehension, conception, and even conjecture. He outstrips the faculties of sight, hearing, and understanding. All the glories that one can sing of him all his life cannot do any justice to him.*

Again:

> *If all the mountains were pounded into ink and mixed with the waters of the oceans and the whole earth were a sheet of paper, one cannot record the greatness of a Guru or Master.*

He is the King of Spirituality, and we, groveling like insects in the muck of the world, cannot know him and his greatness.

Maulana Rumi says:

> *If I were to sing praises of His countless blessings till Eternity, I can hardly say anything of them.*

Whatever we say of him, we perforce do so at an intellectual level, which has a very narrow and limited scope. All our efforts in this direction are bound to discredit him rather than to give him any credit.

Guru Arjan, therefore, says:

> *Thou art a King, and I address Thee as an "Elder-Man";*
> *Far from doing any honor to Thee, I bring Thee discredit.*

The highest and subtlest intellect attempting to describe him is just like a toddler standing before his mother and saying, "Oh darling, I know you!" How much can he know of his parent when he does not know anything of himself? His sweet lisping words cannot do any justice to the deep motherly love and affection that lies in her bosom. We too cannot sing the glories of the Master, for we cannot know, at the bar of the intellect, him who is beyond all barriers and limitations.

Blessed indeed are we, for Master Souls, as and when they do appear, at times tell us of themselves. It is from their rare utterances that we can know something of their greatness and of the potential power that works through them.

In innumerable little ways, in parables and otherwise, they tell us of what they are, what is their mission, from where they come and how they carry out God's Plan.

It would be advisable for us to go to them and listen to what they have to say about themselves.

CHAPTER TWO

Guru is Shabd
(Master is Word Personified)

THE Gospel of John begins with the memorable words:

> *In the beginning was the Word, and the Word was with God, and the Word was God.*
> *The same was in the beginning with God.*
>
> JOHN 1:1-2

Guru is Shabd or Word personified. *The Word was made flesh and dwelt among us,* says the Gospel. Shabd or Word is just a ray from God or the great Ocean of Consciousness, and this one ray is responsible for the creation and sustenance of all the planes comprising the universe.

In the Gospel of John we read further:

> *All things were made by him (i.e., the Word) and without him was not anything made that was made.*
> *In him was life; and the life was the light of men.*
> *And the light shineth in darkness; and the darkness comprehended it not.*
>
> JOHN 1:2-5

Dryden in his poetic fantasy refers to It as Harmony (or Sound Principle):

*From Harmony, from Heavenly Harmony
   This Universal frame began;
Through all the compass of the notes It ran,
   The Diapason closing full in man.*

In Gurbani, we have:

Word is the Master and spirit is the disciple of Word.

Word is the Master and the Prophet, full of wisdom, deep and profound. Without Word, the world cannot exist.

Between Word and the Master, there is no distinction. Word indeed is the Elixir of Life, and whosoever follows the Word according to the instructions of a living Master, safely crosses the ocean of life.

Tulsi Sahib says:

Spirit is the disciple, and Word is the Master. It is only after the spirit is linked with the Word that she finds the way Godward, by rising into the beyond and entering into the inverted well.

Bhai Gurdas speaks of spirit as:

It is only after the spirit faithfully and conscientiously accepts Dhunni (Sound Current or Word) as Master, that she becomes a Gur-

> mukh and knows that the Word and the Master are in fact One.

Saint Kabir likewise thus explains:

> Where is the Master, and where does the spirit dwell? How can the two unite? For without union, spirit has no rest.

He himself then answers:

> Master is in the Gaggan, and so is the seat of the Spirit.
> When the two are united, there is no separation thereafter;
> Accept the Word as Master; all the rest is sham tinsel;
> Each selfishly engaged wanders from place to place.

Thus Word or Shabd is a World Teacher from the beginning of time.

Blessed are the pure in heart, for in them the Word of the Master manifests Itself. This Word is the Real Saint and can act as a living guide. It is "God-in-Action" and is expressed in abundance in Master Souls who are one with God.

> When I churned the sea of body, a strange phenomenon came to Light;
> God was identified in Master, and no distinctinction could Nanak find.

He who is a doer of the Word is called a Saint, or a

Master Soul. This Truth dawns only when one studies the significance of the term *Guru*. It is derived from the Sanskrit root *Giri,* which means *One who calls;* thus he who always hears this call within himself, and is devotedly attached to the call and can make it manifest in others, is described in Gurbani as *Guru.*

> *Accept as Master one who can make Truth manifest;*
> *Give expression to the Inexpressible by means of Sound.*

Again:

> *O Nanak! verily Truth alone is True.*

Kabir Sahib says:

> *We do obeisance to all teachers, whatever their creed;*
> *But the Adept in Sound Principle is greatest indeed.*

Again:

> *Teachers there are of degrees vast in variation,*
> *But the one of Sound Current is for highest adoration.*

Tulsi Sahib also exhorts:

> *He who can reveal Sound Current is verily a Saint;*
> *By analysis of self, one locates the Sound within.*

Kabir Sahib has challenged that whoever calls himself a

Satguru or a Saint should enable us to see the Unmanifest Manifested.

In *Sar Bachan* we have:

> *Master brings the message of Sound; He serves nothing but the Sound;*
> *Perfect Master is ever engaged in Sound; Be thou the dust of the feet of the Master of Sound.*

Satguru is a veritable *Veda*. He is endowed with *Sach Naam* and thus possesses the Elixir of Life. He distributes *Shabd,* which works as an "Open Sesame" to the Heavenly regions and grants free access to pilgrims on the Master's Path.

The Theosophists call It the Voice of the Silence; its reverberations can be heard from plane to plane.

In the terminology of the Masters, a real Saint is one who can teach of Shabd. Without an adept no one can have the gift of Shabd or *Naam*. It may be likened to a rope ladder leading directly to God, and a spirit by taking hold of It can easily ascend Godward.

> *Contact with Shabd is contact with God; and blessed is one who contacts Shabd within.*

Again:

> *God in Guru distributes Shabd; By contact with Truth one merges in Truth.*

And again:

> *O Nanak! all Saints from the beginning are embedded in Shabd;*

> *Blessed is Master Ram Das who too has contacted Shabd.*

In the Holy Bible we have:

> *The Word was made flesh and dwelt among us.*

It is from an adept in Shabd that one gets a true life impulse. He himself is one with that true Life Current, from which everything animate derives life. He is a resident of the egoless region, he is Shabd personified. He lives and has his very being in Shabd, having crossed far beyond the sway of *Kal* or Time; he lives life everlasting and is competent to pass it on to others who contact him and follow his instructions.

The human spirit at present lies buried under an immense load of *mayaic* or material pressure. It does not even know that it is spirit. It can be awakened to Reality and made aware of its greatness only by means of Shabd. This Life Principle of Shabd already lies in each one of us, but only in a latent form.

It has to be made patent or audible to the spirit, so that it may by sheer affinity grow conscious of its rich spiritual heritage and claim it as its own.

This contact of the spirit with Shabd can be brought about and is firmly established by the Master (who is Shabd personified) and no one else can do it.

> *Shabd is a sacred trust with the Master, and is scrupulously discharged;*
> *Shabd of the Master, a Master alone can manifest;*
> *And none else is competent to do so.*

It means that Shabd or Word is under the control of the Master. He alone can manifest It or make It audible by pulling the spirit out of the physical sensory organs.

This contact with Shabd comes as a gracious gift from the Master. No amount of meritorious deeds performed within the limitations of time, space, and causation, can merit such a priceless gift, so vast and so limitless as Shabd:

All our righteousnesses are as filthy rags.

And again:

By works of the law shall no flesh be justified.

The Master may grant the gift of Shabd out of extreme compassion and grace if he so wills.

The moment a helpless child tries to pull himself toward his mother, she fondly runs toward him, tenderly picks him up, and lovingly hugs him to her bosom.

It cannot be had by endeavors nor by service;
But may come when fully reposed without clutching;
Out of the Great Grace of the Lord, one takes to the instructions of the Master.

It does not mean that a person should not try to exert himself. He must on the contrary work zealously according to the Master's instructions. The success, however, depends on the will of the Master alone, for he is the sole arbiter of the manner and measure of His Grace.

Christ said:

If you love me, keep my commandments.

To mold one's life in terms of the Master is a necessity on the path of the Master.

> *He who verily follows the Master is ever engaged in hearing the Divine Music. As the Naam develops, one gets absorbed in it.*

Though this *Anhad Bani* (Ceaseless Sound Current) or *Naam* (Word) is the Life of our life, yet we cannot make It manifest or audible by ourselves; an approach to It is always through a Master Saint or *Ustad-i-Kamil*:

> *Ceaseless Sound is a Treaure within, with an approach through a Saint;*
> *Without a Master, even Sidhs and Sadhaks have failed to get Naam.*

Shabd is the mainstay of Saints as well as of all living creatures, the difference being that of conscious awareness in one case and unconscious ignorance in the other. While the former have not only an experience of "Sonship" but truly live in that relationship, the latter have no idea of it at all.

Christ says:

> *I am the Son of God.*
> *I and my Father are one.*
> *Whatever comes from me comes from my Father.*

In *Gurbani* we also have similar references:

> *Hari (God) does what His Saints wish for.*
> *What they (Saints) desire, that comes to pass; none can deny their wishes.*

> *Father and son are dyed in the same color.*

Maulana Rumi tells us:

> *An Aulia (Godman) is competent enough even to divert a bolt from above.*

It does not mean that Saints in any way question the authority of God, or run a parallel administration of their own. Far from this, they act as agents and hold His Commission. In the world God acts through them.

Egoless as they are, they become fitting instruments of Godly Powers. Allied closely with Shabd, they receive from and transmit direct messages to God; and in relation to the world, they are just polarized God:

> *The Father and the Son are One, and administer the same law.*
>
> *O Paltu! In the domain of God, there is no other manager than a Saint. The two are so closely and indissolubly knit together that the Saint appears to be running the whole show.*

Maulana Rumi speaks of It in this wise:

> *Aulia or Godmen are the chosen of God.*
> *They have full knowledge of all that is visible and invisible.*

Again, God speaks through Saints:

> *O Lalo! I simply speak out what God makes me speak, said Nanak.*
> *Sadh is the mouthpiece of God.*

In the garb of man, God comes into the world for the sake of suffering humanity, and through His Saving Grace He takes upon Himself vicarious responsibilities for their shortcomings:

> *See God descending in thy Human frame;*
> *The Offended, suffering in the offender's name;*
> *All thy misdeeds to Him imputed see,*
> *And all His Righteousness devolv'd on thee.*
>
> DRYDEN

A living Master is the only hope for the erring mankind; a kindly Light to guide their faltering footsteps and a Saviour for the sinful. With the help of limitless Naam or Shabd, of which he is a vast treasure-house, he helps the *jivas* or the embodied spirits to cross safely over the ocean of life and gain Life Eternal.

Inwardly linked and embedded in Shabd, outwardly he works like a Teacher or a Guru and gives spiritual instructions to the aspirants on the physical plane, and then passes on at will to the subtle and the causal planes and beyond, as the jiva progresses on the spiritual path, and guides him at every step. He does not stop until he leaves the *Sadhak* in his native home from where Shabd originates and which, in fact, he is.

One who has known *Sat Purush* (or the Primal Cause), is a *Satguru* (or Master of Truth). He is beyond the sway both of Dissolution (*Kal* or Time) and of Grand Dissolution (*Maha Kal* or Greater Time), and is competent to lead the aspirants to this stage. A

Master of this caliber alone can save the jivas and nobody else can.

> *He Who is One with Truth, is the Master of Truth;*
> *He can liberate spirits and Nanak sings His praises.*

> *More safe and much more modest, 'tis to say;*
> *God would not leave mankind without a way.*

CHAPTER THREE

Gradations in Mastership

MASTERS are of four different types: The father, the mother, the preceptor or teacher, and lastly, *Satguru* (Spiritual Guide or *Murshid-i-Kamil*).

Of all of these, *Satguru* is the greatest teacher, for he imparts spiritual instructions alone. One who is well-versed in worldly wisdom is called *acharya* or preceptor, for he gives us rules of social conduct and of ethical life.

Satguru or Master of Truth is also known as *Sant Satguru*. His relation with his disciples is purely a spiritual one, as he is concerned with the advancement of spirit and has nothing to do with worldly matters.

From the viewpoint of spiritual attainments *Gurus* may be classified as:

Sadh Guru,
Sant Satguru, and
Param Sant Satguru.

A *Sadh* is one who has gone beyond the region of *Trikuti* (*Onkar*) which is the same as *Lahut* in Sufi terminology and *Hu* in Islamic theology. He has witnessed the spirit in its pristine glory, after having rid it of all coverings, and is now *Trigunatit* (*beyond* the three gunas: *Satva, Rajas,* and *Tamas,* in which all human beings work according to their natural and native instincts); *beyond* the five elements (earth, water, fire, air and ether, of which the physical world is composed); *beyond* the twenty-five *Prakritis* (the subtle forms in varying degrees of the elements); and *beyond* also mind and matter.

In short, he is an adept in self-knowledge, or the art and science of spirit, and can, at will, disengage the spirit from various *koshas* (sheaths or caskets) in which it is enclosed like a priceless gem.

The greatness of a Sadh lies beyond the three gunas (as he is Trigunatit).

By a process of self-analysis, he (a *Sadh*) has known the self or spirit in its real form—to wit, that it is of the same essence as God; and now he strives for God-knowledge.

A *Sant* is one who is adept not only in self-knowledge but in God-knowledge as well. He far transcends the material, materio-spiritual, and spirituo-material realms. Master of Truth as he is, his abode is in the purely spiritual region, technically called *Sach Khand* or *Muqam-i-Haq,* the Realm of Truth.

A *Param Sant* is the Grand Master of Truth beyond all description and hence ineffable. He is at one with what is variously known as *Anami* (The Namless One) of Kabir; *Nirala* (Indescribably Wonderful), *Mahadayal* (Boundless Mercy) or *Swami* (The Great Lord of All).

There is no material difference between a *Sant* and a *Param Sant* except in nomenclature.

But none of them, whether a *Sadh,* a *Sant,* or a *Param Sant,* can act or function as a Guru or Master unless he is competent to impart spiritual instructions and he has been commissioned from above to do this work. Whoever holds this authority for spiritual work becomes a *Sadh Guru, Sant Guru,* or *Param Sant Guru,* as the case may be.

There may be a number of *Sadhs, Sants* or *Param Sants,* but none of them can of himself assume Guruship or spiritual preceptorship without being commissioned for the work.

So the terms *Sadh, Sant* and *Param Sant* have a much wider connotation than the term *Guru,* which is restricted to a spiritual preceptor alone—the rest being only spiritual adepts of varying degrees.

The Guru holds a direct commission from God, and works under instructions just as any vice-regent would do on behalf of a king.

Again Gurus are of two types:

1. *Swateh Sant Gurus*: They are born *Sants* who come into the world with direct commissions; as for instance, Kabir Sahib and Guru Nanak.

They start the work of spiritual knowledge and instructions right from a tender age. They need no special training from anyone, since they come from the Most High for this purpose. Such beings, when they come, simply flood the world with the light of Spirituality, and establish a line of *Gurmukh Gurus* for carrying on the work long after them. But in course of time, substance comes to be sacrificed for show, and gradually Spirituality disappears altogther.

Then comes another Master Soul to re-orient this

most ancient science according to the needs of the age. In this way, "old wine" remains in circulation for souls athirst. Such Master Souls do appear from time to time in different lands and among different peoples.

2. Besides *Swateh Sants* there are *Sants* who by devotional practice and spiritual discipline under the guidance of some Master Soul acquire spiritual merit here and are granted a commission to work as a Guru.

They already have a rich spiritual background ripe for fruition, and in the present span of life simply seem to complete the process. *Gurmukhs* are always in the making from life to life, and acquire perfection in this life.

> *Kabir saith that he came directly from the Kingdom of God and held an instrument of instructions from Him.*

Bhai Gurdas, while speaking of Guru Nanak, tells us:

> *First he got a commission and then he worked it out.*

In short, the former come with authority, and the latter acquire authority while here. But there is absolutely no difference between the greatness of the two, the nature and scope of their work and the method by which the work is executed. Each of them is endowed with equal authority, and works out the grand plan of God according to the needs of the time and of the people.

But the rest who claim this status and pose and act as Master Souls not only deceive themselves but misguide the masses at large. In this category are included persons who are either greedy and selfish or those who are after name and fame.

In innumerably different ways and wiles they practice deception on the unwary and simple-minded seekers after Truth with a view to serve their own ends.

It is because of such impositions that Guruship is being looked down upon by most people, and no wonder that the science of Spirituality is being stigmatized as a mirage and a fool's paradise.

CHAPTER FOUR

Guru: One or Many

SHABD or Word (the Primal Sound Current) is the only Guru for the entire world and *Surat* (individual consciousness) is the only disciple, as the latter cannot do without the former. In fact, there is the principle of unity, for God is One, though He has manifested Himself variously.

But as we look the other way and turn to the world abounding in diverse forms, we see a Pole-star shining in its majesty reflecting the Light of Heaven.

Such a pure soul (Word made flesh or Godman) with authority to give spiritual instructions to the seekers after God, is as much a Guru as the Shabd Itself, for he himself is a living embodiment of Shabd and with Shabd as stock in trade freely distributes It to whomever he likes.

Kabir speaks of himself:

I come from the Kingdom of God to administer the Law of God.

Guru Nanak, too, was invested with a similar authority to impart spiritual instructions when he was in deep meditation in *Veiny Nadi* (the Water of Spirituality within).

Both of them were Param Sant Satgurus.

Kabir Sahib was born in 1398 A.D. at Lahr Talao near Benaras and passed away in 1518. Guru Nanak was born in 1469 A.D. at Talwandi, and left the physical plane at Kartarpur in 1539. Thus both of them were contemporaries for about forty-nine years, from 1469 to 1518. In the same way Shamas-i-Tabrez and Maulana Rumi were also contemporaries for some time.

Again, Guru Angad and Dadu Sahib lived together from 1504 to 1552.

So also, Guru Arjan and Dharam Das from 1561 to 1606.

These instances go to show that there can be more than one Guru at the same time, but a person cannot have more than one Guru for spiritual perfection. It does not matter even if a Guru after initiating a person passes away.

Once he initiates an individual, the Subtle Form of the Master gets embedded in the disciple for he becomes from that moment the disciple's ideal and his instructions gradually begin to bear fruit.

There is no power on earth that can render sterile the seed sown by a Master Soul. Master never dies. He may leave the body, as anyone else does, but he is more than a mere body. He is an ideal, a living Sound Current or a Life Principle that gives Life and Light to the entire world.

After his passing away one may derive benefit from the *Satsang* conducted by a *Gurmukh* who is carrying on the duties of Guru, and may consult him in case he has some difficulty. It is, however, of the utmost importance that the Master is not to be changed on any account.

Loyalty to the Master who has initiated the spirit and to whom the spirit has pledged his troth demands the recognition that the Master is competent to impart further guidance and instructions, even when he is working on the spiritual plane after having left the physical world.

CHAPTER FIVE

Present Master

MASTER OF THE TIME is a living Master who is imparting spiritual instructions to his following. But all Masters of bygone times are *past Masters* or Masters out of date. Each of these Masters had his own role to perform. The accounts of the ancient and outdated Masters and their teachings do a kind of spadework by cutting the untrodden soil and by creating an interest in us in esoteric matters of the spirit. Each of them lays emphasis on the need of the living Master and records his own spiritual experiences. It is from their exhortations that we are moved to begin the search. The innate urge in us is quickened and we are impelled to go in quest of one who can lead us Godward.

The work of imparting actual spiritual instructions and guidance is, however, done by a living Master. Highly charged as he is with higher consciousness, he injects the jivas with his life impulse. Spirituality can neither be bought nor taught, but it may be *caught,* like an infection from one highly infected himself. As Light comes from Light, so Life comes from Life, and a spirit that is bodily ridden can only be moved by a Spirit that is untrammelled by body and mind. This is the only way and there is no other way for spiritual training.

Without a living Master there can be no escape from bondage for the spirit.

Maulana Rumi, therefore, emphatically declares:

> *Trust not thy learning, cunning, and craft;*
> *Do not break away from the sheet anchor of the Living Prophet.*

Prophet Mohammed, too, says:

> *He who has not sincerely approached the Immam of the Time (living Master), the Vice-Regent of Allah, the Perfect Guide, cannot get anything.*

Again, the Great Maulana said:

> *Hie to thy God through the Godman:*
> *Float not uselessly on the treacherous waters of egoism.*

In the absence of a living Master, one cannot develop the devotional attitude so very necessary on the spiritual path. There cannot be any devoted attachment for a person or thing which we have never seen and of which we have no idea. The very term "attachment" signifies that there is an object of attachment.

Some persons feel that this need for an approach to a living Master so emphatically stressed in *Gurbani* related to the time of the ten Gurus alone, but that is not the case. The teachings of the Masters were addressed to man in general and were for all times. Their appeal was universal and not restricted to any particular sect or any specific period:

> *The teachings of the Masters are common for all.*

Again:

> *Bani (Word or Sound Principle) is the Guru, and Guru is the Bani personified, and the Elixir of Life gushes out of the Bani.**
>
> *Whoever accepts what the Gurbani says, he can be freed through the grace of the living Master.*

Bhai Gurdas in this context says:

> *The Vedas and scriptures are the wares of the Masters and help in crossing the ocean of life; but without the Master of Truth coming down and living among us, we cannot apprehend the Reality.*

The esoteric mysteries cannot be fully explained in writing, as the inner process has its own difficulties and handicaps. In various ways the Master in his Subtle Form helps the spirit in the journey from plane to plane. This work of guidance both within and without cannot be performed by past Masters.

---

* There is a vast difference between *Gurbani* and *Bani*. The former refers to the sayings of the Gurus as recorded in the holy scriptures (especially the *Granth Sahib*), whereas the latter refers to the eternal Sound Current, sometimes called *Gur-ki-Bani,* reverberating in all creation. It emanates from God Himself and He alone can manifest it. Moreover, this Bani (Naam or Word) is sounding throughout the four *Yugas* (ages) and gives its message of Truth.

The nameless and formless *Shabd* becomes a form and assumes a name and dwells among us. In the Holy Gospel we have:

The Word became flesh and dwelt among us.

Unless God comes down in the garb of man, we cannot know the Unknowable. The teachings of scriptures remain sealed to us under the heavy weight of ancient and archaic verbiage, unless a Master Soul who has actual experience of the Science of the Spirit explains to us the truth of these scriptures.

Even the apparently simple teachings of the late Masters fail to yield the right import unless some living adept in the line tells us their true significance, and makes us experience the same experiences mentioned in the scriptures.

By transmitting his own life impulse, he enlivens the spirit lying helplessly shrivelled in the body under the dead weight of mind and matter. Like a clever guide, he, in an inimitable way of his own, quietly gives her a new lead.

Next, he lays bare to the spirit's view new heavens full of wondrous sights, charters her a plane (*Shabd*) and pilots her Godward himself. From day to day the spirit is wheeled around sharp corners, touches new spots, experiences unknown thrills, and enjoys exhilarating experiences too subtle to be described.

All this and much more is the work that a living Master has to do.

In the history of Sikhism, we find that the Holy

Granth was compiled for the first time by the fifth Guru, Guru Arjan. In spite of the well-known and oft-quoted dictum that *Bani is the Guru,* implying thereby that there was no need of Gurus thereafter, the Gurus carried on the work of initiating people; and even today the *Khalsa* (Pure One) with perfect, resplendent Light within is authorized to carry on the work of spiritual instruction and guidance to seekers after Truth.

Guru Gobind Singh says: *We are the worshipers of the Great Conscious Light* and defines the word *Khalsa* as: *The pure Khalsa is one in whom the Light of God is fully manifested.* He further goes on to say:

*Khalsa is my true form; I reside in Khalsa,
He is the life of my life, and my very prana
(vital airs);
Khalsa is my valiant friend, Khalsa is my Satguru Pura (fully competent Master);
I have told no untruth.
I tell this in the presence of Par Brahm and
Guru Nanak.*

CHAPTER SIX

The Need of a Master

THE FORMLESS GOD pervades the Universe in the form of Shabd or Word; but we cannot feel blessed unless we are enabled to contact It within.

The entire atmosphere is charged with electricity but one cannot derive any benefit from it so long as one cannot reach out to an electric switch that controls the energy coming from the power-house.

Once this contact is established, it gives us light, hot or cold breezes as we may need, and helps us in innumerable ways in sweeping the house, cooking our food and the like. It carries huge industrial loads like the proverbial demon and does work that a thousand persons put together cannot do.

In exactly the same way, if one could but reach out to some human pole where God's energy in the form of Shabd is manifest, one can become truly blessed and reap a rich spiritual harvest beyond all measure. Saints, prophets, seers, and Master Souls are such manifested poles that radiate God's Light, Life and Love.

They are the Children of Light and come to give Light to the world which is steeped in utter darkness. They are Shabd personified and, so to say, polarized God within the world.

> *Holy men of God spake as they were moved by the Holy Ghost.*
>
> II PETER 1:21
>
> *The spirit of the Lord spake by me, and his Word was in my tongue.*
>
> II SAMUEL 23:2
>
> *Thy Word is a lamp unto my feet and a Light unto my path.*
>
> PSALM 119:105

Satguru or Master of Truth is then the pole wherefrom God's energy works for the Divine Will. This energy or Shabd is the Subtlest Form of the Great Unknown and the Unknowable. It is through the Satguru that one can know even this much and come into contact with Shabd.

It is from the physical that we move to the subtle. The Master and the Master's Sound Current are the means to the end. They alone can lead the spirit Godward. The Master solves for us the mystery of God and saves us from the tentacles of mind and matter.

His long and strong arm pulls a spirit out of body and mind consciousness and makes it Spirit Consciousness by linking it with the Sound Principle.

The Radiant Music next leads the spirit to the source or region from which It is emanating. The Master and the Sound Current are not two different entities; they are but two aspects of the same thing.

As he works on the physical plane, he has to assume and work through a physical vehicle, without which spiritual instruction cannot be imparted. But as soon as he disengages a human spirit from the various sheaths and coatings, he also assumes and works through a subtle Form—luminous and resplendent.

This process goes on until the spirit of man becomes identical with that of the Master. This is the grand purpose for the fulfilment of which Masters come into this lowest region which is so full of misery and woe. Armed with the Saving Grace of God, in the form of the Holy Ghost—variously called *Shabd,* Word, *Naad, Bani* or *Kalma*—the Master saves such souls as are ripe for redemption, listen to him, and work out their salvation by following his instructions.

Unless God comes in the garb of man and dwells among us, we cannot know of God in spite of His immanent presence everywhere.

Someone must churn clarified butter from milk, and strike fire out of the granite blocks, before we can know that butter is hidden in milk and fire in stone. "Word," therefore, becomes flesh and dwells among us, as we learn from the Holy Gospel.

When spirits grow restless from their long exile into the physical plane, helplessly cry out for homecoming and see no way out of the clutches of Kal's all pervading limitations of time, space, and causation, the Saving Grace of God is stirred by the piteous appeals and comes into the world in the form of a Sant Satguru (Master of Truth) to help them out of the impasse.

It is the living Master who can do this job. No one else can. It is through the Voice of the Silence that He speaks. His is an unwritten law and an unspoken language.

Scriptures, however sacred and authoritative, contain bare references to spiritual regions and record the experiences of their authors, but can neither impart spiritual instruction nor be a guide on the spiritual path.

The Word of the Master works as an "Open Sesame" to the heavenly regions. He holds the key that unlocks the Kingdom of God, now a lost province to us. It is out of compassion and love for the lost sheep that the Shepherd comes out of his fold, treads the stony path in an endless search, picking up lost souls here and there.

> *I am the light of the world: he that followeth me shall not walk in darkness, but shall have the light of life.*
>
> JOHN 8:12

CHAPTER SEVEN

Past Saints

TODAY a person who is ill cannot have the benefit of medical advice from Dhanwantri (the progenitor of medical science), nor can a litigant ask Solomon to decide his case, nor can a lady marry Adonis and bring forth children.

Similarly, Saints who appeared in the past from time to time and conferred spiritual benefit on those who came into contact with them, cannot do anything for the present generation. Each had his commission, and on completing it, entrusted the work of regeneration to his successor. Man can learn only from man, and God works His ways through living Saints.

> *Surely the Lord God will do nothing, but he revealeth his secret unto his servants the prophets.*
>
> AMOS 3:7

Some people think that past *Mahatmas* continue to live in spiritual regions and can even now confer spiritual benefit on the aspirants. Let us see how this holds good in the light of reason:

1. Each Saint has his mission in life and comes with a definite instrument of instruction. As soon as he completes his job, he retires from this world (physical plane)

and goes back into the Spiritual Ocean from which he sprang, leaving the work of further reorientation to his successor.

2. Again, in accordance with the Law of Nature, even if the predecessor has had to do something for his followers, he does it through the living successor to whom he entrusted the work on retirement; and only the latter, as a brother-in-faith or *Gur-bhai* may help and guide his brethren on the physical plane.

3. It is only when we are able to leave the physical plane at will or at the time of death that we can contact the Master who initiated us if he has left the body. Even while living on this earth his resplendent and luminous form never comes down from the *Gaggan* (astral heaven), for he always awaits human spirits at the threshold of the materio-spiritual regions.

4. Again, in the hope and belief that the ancient Saints and sages can even now help us, we begin to attach great importance to ill-shaped and ill-formed currents and undercurrents of thought and feelings, and try to work on the suggestions of our own subconscious mind, little understanding its true import, and taking for granted that the impressions are from this or that past Master.

These manifestations may even have been stirred up by some agency other than that of our *Isht Dev,* or the past Master of our choice. This cannot be seen in its proper perspective unless one is first gifted with inner vision (*Divya Drishti*), which can successfully penetrate through the veil of mind and matter and see clearly and judge correctly the nature of the ill-conceived inner urges, as they swim up indistinctly to the mental surface.

5. Alongside the above, we cannot possibly understand the working of a prophet whom we have never met and seen with our eyes, nor have we the means to verify his *modus operandi*. In these circumstances, we can easily be deluded by any wandering spirit or will-of-the-wisp, or may even fall easy prey to the Negative Power, with its diverse ways of enticing untrained souls.

6. If, for instance, it may for the moment be admitted that the ancient sages can still lead us on the spiritual path and the present Master is not needed for spiritual instructions, then the very idea of having a *Guru* at any time in the past or present is at once eliminated, for God can directly teach man easily without any prophet or Messiah.

7. The very fact that a sage or seer appeared at one time or another and helped people Godward is in itself proof, conclusive and positive, even in this age, that there is need of such a Godman; for without him one cannot know of God or move Godward.

8. God by Himself can teach man only by becoming man, for man alone can teach man. He has perforce to put on the garb of man—call him what you will: a *Sadh, Sant,* prophet, *Messiah* or *Rasul. Like attracts like* is an incontrovertible dictum.

God appears as a Sadh.

God takes on the appellation of Sant.

This does not mean at all that past Masters are dead and gone. Far from it; they have attained Immortality. Having finally traversed the physical, the subtle, and the causal planes, they are at One with the Cosmic Awareness. If with all their devotion and spiritual advancement, they were still to wander under the moon, they would have wasted all their endeavors.

It will not serve any useful purpose to enter into theoretical discussion and disputation. Everything will become clear if one searches for a real Master, well versed in the art and science of spirit, and learns from him an easy and natural way of approach to God.

There will be no need to wait for the result until death. If the seed is sown properly and watered, the fruit must appear quickly and in abundance in one's very lifetime.

A living Master can grant eternal beatitude in its fullness. A simple touch with the dynamic power of the higher consciousness in him is enough to charge one with the radiating waves of spirituality. The spirit is drawn inward and upward and riding the magnetic-like radiant strains, crosses from plane to plane. Blessed indeed is the spirit that contacts such a Master and comes under his protection.

It is a matter of common experience that a person bound for any foreign country consults directories, collects data about shipping companies, the various boats scheduled by each, the facilities they offer, the ports of embarkation and call, the route that each boat would follow, and the time that each would take, the places of interest on the way, and ultimately where he would stay on reaching the destination.

After having laid his plans, he has to obtain a passport from his own government, without which he cannot leave his country; and he also has to arm himself with a landing permit from the government of the country to which he is bound.

In exactly the same way, a person who intends to leave the physical plane for any of the spiritual planes has to obtain a passport and a landing permit from some competent authority, some vice-regent of God (a Saint), who works on all the planes.

This is granted to him at the time of Initiation, when acquainting him with the various ports of call on the way, the different signs and signals wherewith to distinguish and recognize each place, the difficulties of the journey and the like. In this way, he grants the traveler the necessary passport, and a landing permit for disembarkation. Once the seed of Naam is sown in a jiva, it cannot but fructify, and he must one day reach the Kingdom of God, the Garden of Eden, from which he has been an exile from time immemorial. And no power here or beyond can stand in the way of his homecoming.

The next thing the Master does is lay down the correct path that leads to God. Like a veteran seaman, he plans the entire route for the traveler, as without it he cannot, with all of his sincere devotion and steadfast effort, reach the destination.

The correct lead Godward is the second preparatory stage for this venture on the unknown seas. The Master himself charters the boat and underwrites the disciple's safety *en route,* by telling him of the shoals and the submerged rocks in the way and other dangers besetting the journey, and how best to avoid them.

He does not stop here. Master of both Heaven and Earth, he every day traverses at will the various spiritual regions. *Sach Khand* or *Muqam-i-Haq* is his perpetual abode from where he comes down every day to the earth plane, to discharge the lowliest duties cast on him.

Type of the wise, who soar, but never roam;
True to the kindred points of Heaven and Home.

Since he has a personal knowledge and actual experience of the journey which he performs so often every day, and is a resident of the highest plane, he gives a cheery call to the world-weary:

Come ye all, my unhappy brothers and sisters, into the Kingdom of Heaven and into the Gracious Presence.

He not only gives us first-hand knowledge of the Kingdom of God, plans our itinerary for the journey and books our passage homeward, but also offers to accompany us and be our guide. He may even pilot us, and does not rest content until he escorts us to the mansions of the Lord.

We can verify for ourselves some salient features of the account given by him, by reference to the directories; and should the latter seem to support him in broad outline we take courage and depend on him and his competency with confidence.

The scriptures are nothing but directories which record the personal experiences of those sages and seers who in the past traveled on this path, and a living Master refers to them in his talks and discourses simply because we by nature have dogmatic faith in them, and he wants to take us up from the line of least resistance.

We may break the arid ground by careful study of scriptures, but these *per se* cannot help in liberating the spirit from body and mind consciousness, and in leading her across to the spiritual regions. It is the strong and long arm of the living Master that can accomplish this Herculean task of cleansing the Augean stables, of carrying the spirit beyond all limitations and concepts, and steering her course safely and getting back for her the lost Kingdom.

> *It is the fundamental Law of God that no one can think of Him unless he is reminded of Him by some Master Soul.*
>
> NANAK

Bhai Gurdas says:

> *Endless queries, without treading the Path, cannot lead thee to thy Beloved.*

One cannot understand God by means of intellect alone, however sharp and keen it may be. How can an instrument by nature limited in its scope measure the Limitless? Some higher consciousness can lead the little consciousness to the Great Consciousness, for he serves as link between the two:

> *If one could reach God alone, why then the pangs of separation?*
> *Meet Him through a Sadh, and have beatitude, O Nanak.*
>
> *A quest in the wrong direction cannot lead to success. O Kabir, take with thee a guide and find the great jewel. A sure guide will help thee to reach the goal quickly, however distant it may seem to be.*

We feel the need of a teacher at every step. A student in cookery, for instance, has to learn it from one expert in the culinary art. A student in medicine has to seek the aid of a professor of medicine. A novice in surgery has to master the art from some reputed surgeon, and so also a pupil in engineering, painting, and so forth. Books and learned treatises on these various subjects cannot by themselves make a student expert in the subject.

It is the practical demonstration, the experiment at the table, and the actual operation in the theater under the guidance of an adept in the profession that matters.

If all of these physical sciences that belong to the realm of *Apara Vidya* and are studied and mastered on the plane of the senses require the help of a teacher, the need of a teacher is still greater for spiritual science (*Para Vidya*), which is an inner process far beyond the ken of the senses, to be studied in the depths of the mind and experimented with in the laboratory of the soul.

It has been locked up for ages upon ages and is enshrouded in stark darkness and there is no visible approach to it. The fact is that a person who denies and derides the necessity of a Master in Truth and yet wants to learn Truth all by himself does not in fact want it. His case is just like that of a man who prefers to dig a well for himself rather than quench his thirst at a spring of cool and refreshing water nearby, with a waterman ready to serve him.

Bhai Nandlal says in this context:

None but a lover of rubies can understand the value of a ruby.
It is only the jeweler's eyes that can at a glance give value to it.

The need of a Guru or Master is absolute, and there can be no exception to the rule. Suppose, for instance, a person wants to have a joy-ride in the air. No one will allow him to enter a plane by himself. Even if he enters it surreptitiously, he will find the machinery locked. If somehow or other he overcomes this obstacle, he will not know how to handle the various parts of the machine. Should he dabble with it and the plane starts, he cannot take it up for want of necessary training, nor can he bring it down, nor steer it correctly. The result, sooner or later, will be a crash and loss of life. The mechanism of the human body is much more complicated and delicate than that of any machine; therefore the need of a spiritual adept is all the greater, both for success in the practical process of self-analysis and also for the approach to God Himself and the understanding of the working of the divine Will.

The spirit imprisoned in the body cannot *per se* separate itself from it. With its seat above the focus of the eyes, it permeates the entire sysem, and the two are indissolubly intertwined with each other. Should it somehow or other find itself freed momentarily and collected and gathered up at its center, it cannot enter the airliner of Shabd. If it may find a way in, it does not know where to go, how to go, and how to return.

But if the master pilot (the Sant Satguru) could be there to take the spirit along with him, and the two could enter the plane and take a few joyful rides together in the spiritual realm, the spirit could also learn how to handle the heavenly liner, and to repeat the spiritual experiments.

One well-versed in the mechanism of the human body (which is composed of three coverings: physical, mental, and causal, plus the living sentient entity underneath), a habitual traveler to the heavenly regions, day in and day out, can initiate a spirit into the mysteries of spiritual knowledge, and by a practical demonstration show her a "Way Out."

By actual guidance and help, the Master himself steers her safely from plane to plane, and explains on the way the dangerous signals and points, sharp turns and twists, and the dangers of the unknown and untrodden spiritual realms. Blessed indeed is the spirit that comes across such an adept in the science and art of Spirituality.

Nothing but ill luck would dog a spirit's footsteps if

she were to spurn his offer and attempt the divine journey by herself, unattended and unaided by a Master Soul.

Maulana Rumi, therefore, in no ambiguous terms warns against such a course:

> *Find a Master Spirit, for without his active help and guidance this journey is beset with untold fears, perils, and dangers.*

In essence, Naam or *Dhun Atmic Shabd* (Word) is an unwritten law in an unspoken language, and, hence, It cannot be had from scriptures and other holy books. This wealth can be obtained only from some adept in Naam, for he is Word personified. He alone is competent to make It manifest to the spirit, and no one else can.

> *It is a fundamental Law of God that none can manifest Naam except Satguru (Master of Truth).*
>
> *The Shabd of a Master Soul can be heard only through His Grace, and no one else can even make It manifest.*

A Master of Truth is fully conversant with all the mysteries of spirituality; hence his testimony carries weight and his charged words drive home and prove effective.

> *Listen to the true and infallible testimony of Saints, for they have a first-hand experience of what they say.*

Gurbani also in unambiguous terms emphatically declares the imperative necessity of a Master Soul. The embodied spirits for ages upon ages have been leading a life of the senses, and have never known that there is another side of the picture as well. Truth can neither be known nor experienced except through the grace of a Master of Truth.

> *Without a Master no one ever found Truth in the past nor in the present. The Crest Jewel of Naam has been kept in the hands of a Master, and He is competent to manifest the same in the jivas.*
>
> *It is through God's Grace that one comes across a Master of Truth. After a spirit has passed through cycles of births, then the Master makes her hear the Sound Current.*
>
> *Listen ye all with attention and learn that there is none so great a philanthropist as a Satguru; for he bestows upon jivas the gift of precious Naam. Those who are prepared to lose their lives (i.e., come above the physical life of the senses), shall find Truth on contacting a Master Soul.*

All Saints with one accord declare that without a Godman, one cannot reach God and attain Godhead. God Himself made this abundantly clear:

> *It is a cardinal principle of God that one cannot even think of Him without the Grace of a Satguru.*

> *Nanak has learned from God that one cannot gain salvation without the active aid of a Master.*

Satguru is a great ophthalmologist and an expert eye surgeon. We are all stark blind. God is within us, and darkly we grope for Him without. But a contact with a Satguru restores to us the lost vision and we begin to realize and experience God in the laboratory of the human mind:

> *The entire mankind is blind and is blindly engaged in deeds of darkness, and finds not a Way out. O Nanak! when a spirit meets a Master of Truth, she begins to see with her own eyes (inner, of course) and she realizes the Truth in the depths of the soul.*

We are nothing short of truly blind, for we see not, regardless of physical eyes. Blindness consists not in the loss of eyes, but in keeping away from God. Nanak says:

> *Call them not blind who have no eyes, O Nanak!*
> *Such in fact are blind who see not the Light of God.*

Guru Arjan tells us that even a person with eyes may yet be blind, if he sees not God Who is the very soul of his soul, and thus he commits sins:

> *A person in full possession of his senses may yet be blind; if he considers that God, the*

> *very Soul of his soul, is far removed from him, and thereby he shamelessly engages in evil.*

With physical eyes we witness the physical world around us. But the *Shiv Netra* or Third Eye in each one of us is closed. When this eye opens, we can see the wonders of the subtle and causal worlds, and even those of the purely spiritual world beyond these:

> *Blind is one who performs deeds of blindness, because his inner eye is closed.*

All of us are concerned with matter, and know not if there is anything else.

> *Ever engaged in mind and matter, he does not even think of God;*
> *Bound for Hades, he is ever in perpetual misery;*
> *Blind and deaf, he does not see beyond;*
> *A slave of the mind, he is immersed in sins.*

It is impossible for anyone to enter the higher regions by his individual efforts. It is imperative for an aspirant of these to take with him an adept who daily treads the sun and moon in his heavenly journeys.

Maulana Rumi says:

> *A person desirous of making a pilgrimage should take with him an experienced pilgrim for the purpose—no matter whether*

> *that pilgrim be a Hindu, a Turk, or an Arab.*

The Satguru, like a master surgeon, can restore vision to the inner eye.

Shamas-i-Tabrez tells us:

> *Should you like to see God, apply the dust of a Godman's feet to thine eye, for he can give sight even to the born blind.*

Naam or Shabd is the collyrium that makes a person capable of seeing heavenly visions. Without Its use one forever remains blind, and human birth avails him not:

> *Without contact with Shabd, a person is both blind and deaf, and gains naught from human birth.*
> *The greatest asset is the blessed Bani, which restores the sight that can apprehend God.*
>
> NANAK

God is permeating through and through, but we do not see Him, as we suffer from myopic vision:

> *Accursed is the person who sees him not, though He is within;*
> *All persons, O Tulsi, suffer from cataract over their eyes.*

Eyes are a great blessing. Without them a person gropes in the dark. The whole physical world is just a blank sheet to a blind person. But how grateful would he feel if some expert surgeon were to restore his sight by means of an operation.

The inner eye is a thousand times more useful than the outer one, as without it one cannot see anything beyond the physical plane, and for ages upon ages he has been blindly staggering, ever since the dawn of creation. The Master of Truth bestows vision to this third eye that has long been lying sealed as it were by constant disuse. Is it not a pity that such a valuable organ should be rendered useless, and that we have not taken the time even to think of the helpless state in which we are? Such indeed is the overpowering influence of mind and matter upon the embodied spirit.

It is not only human beings, but also the gods that stand in need of Light for the third eye, for without It they, too, cannot see anything beyond themselves and their surroundings. Located as they are in the descending order, one below the other, they cannot even see their own Mother—*Shakti* (Energy)—from which each of them has sprung.

> *The entire creation is born of Shakti (Energy), which works through three distinct agencies: Brahma (Creator); Vishnu (Sustainer); and Shiva (Destroyer). Though all three are under her direction and control, yet strange as it may seem, they know her not.*

Tulsi Sahib also tells us that none can safely cross the sea of life except through the Grace of a Guru:

> *None has ever crossed the fearful stream of life*

except with the aid of a Guru, no matter if he may have been an intellectual giant, like Shankara.

When great personages like these stand in need of guidance and help of a Guru, the puny child of clay simply cannot do without a Master Soul.

Without a beneficent Guru no one finds a way out, although he may perform myriads of charitable works and deeds of merit.

Again, Tulsi Sahib says:

Tulsi, without the aid of some Murshid-i-Kamil (perfect Master), you cannot have salvation nor can you see the way thereto.

In *Gurbani* we find emphatic reference to the need for a Guru:

Let there not be the least doubt in the mind of any, for none has ever crossed the tempestuous and fretful seas of life without a Guru.

The world is a fearful ocean. The Word of the Guru is the boat, and he is the captain thereof. It is with his grace that one can reach God, and there is no other way.

Guru is at once the barque and the captain, and without him none can cross. God is the veritable gift of Guru, and the way to salvation lies through Him.

In the scriptures of the Hindus also, we find many such references. In Katha Upanishad I:ii, we have:

> *Very few indeed are the persons who have the good fortune to hear of God, and fewer still who can know of Him. Blessed is the high souled one who talks of Him, and blessed are they who have access to such a personage, and truly blessed is he who with his help and guidance finds God within him.*
>
> *Mere thinking and contemplation are of no avail. Without Initiation one cannot know of God. Unless you learn of God from some Master Soul, you shall not experience Him. He is so subtle that thoughts fail to reach Him and intellect cannot apprehend Him.*

In Chandogya Upanishad IV:ix-3, we have:

> *From the pious and the holy who are just like Gurus, we have heard that without a Master Soul we can neither know nor experience the true nature of the Self.*

In Mandukya Upanishad (I Mandukya, Khand 2, Shalok 7:12), we read:

> *It behooves a Brahmin to disengage himself from the desires for the fruits of Karmas and acquire a spirit of detachment, for God is self-existent and cannot be attracted by deeds of merit. To know Him, he must, like a true seeker and disciple, go to a Guru who*

is adept in the knowledge of Brahma and is fully embedded in Brahma.

Without a Guru one cannot even have true import of the scriptures. In Svetasvatara Upanishad VI:23, it is recorded:

He who is extremely devoted to God and has the same amount of devotion for his Guru, he alone can understand the significance of the text herein.

Let us now turn to Manusmriti, Chapter II:

A disciple must stand before his Guru in perfect equipoise, with full control over his body and bodily organs.

SH. 192

A disciple must everyday before the commencement of his daily lessons and after completion of the same do obeisance at the feet of his Guru and act according to his instructions.

SH. 71

Those who try to follow the Vedas on hearsay authority only, do a great disservice to the Vedas—for none can truly learn the Vedas without a Guru—and such go to hell.

SH. 116

Whosoever imparts to you knowledge either exoteric or esoteric is worthy of your respect.

SH. 117

In Bhagavad Gita IV:34, we have:

> *The practice (of spirituality) can best be done at the feet of a Master Soul, fully conversant with the Reality, for such alone can guide properly.*

We cannot know the spiritual path without the help of a Godman and our search should, therefore, begin with the latter. In the Holy Gospel, it is said:

> *No man cometh unto the Father, but by me.*
> JOHN 14:6

> *No man knoweth . . . who the Father is, but the Son and he to whom the Son will reveal him.*
> LUKE 10:22

> *No man can come to me except the Father which hath sent me draw him.*
> JOHN 6:44

> *He that receiveth you receiveth me, and he that receiveth me receiveth him that sent me.*
> MATTHEW 10:40

In short, the sacred books of all religions repeat the same thing; to wit, that man cannot gain salvation except through a Master of Truth.

The Shastras, the Vedas and the Smritis all converge at one point: no one can have salvation except through grace. Right contemplation will bring home this universal Truth to you as well.

The easiest and the quickest way to reach God is through devotion to some Master Soul. The Prophet of Arabia, while exhorting Ali, said:

> *O Ali! thou art a lion in the cause of Truth, brave and steadfast, but depend not on thy prowess and strength. Far better it would be for thee to take shelter under a tree laden with flowers and fruits.*
>
> *O Ali! of all the ways leading to God, choose one that is of the Beloved of God, for long and strong is his arm and he can easily take the seekers after Truth into His Holy Presence.*

Maulana Rumi also exhorts in the same fashion:

> *The ever oscillating mind cannot be stilled unless it comes under the overpowering influence of some Saint. Should you come across one, take hold of him with a firm grasp. Take rest under the shelter of an accepted one, for the proximity of a liberated Soul shall liberate thee as well.*
>
> *Dove-like sigh thou night and day and search for the hidden treasure from some darvesh (man of God).*

Again:

> *There is no Friend greater than Satguru; He is the protector here and everywhere.*
>
> *Search for such a one right and left, high and low, and never rest until he is found.*

> *Never turn away from the holy and pious, but diligently try to understand them and their real greatness.*

The path of spirituality is strewn with dangers and difficulties and cannot be safely trod except with the help and guidance of a Master.

Every soul is clothed in three distinct sheaths; the physical, the astral, and the causal. It is through each of these that she can operate in the three corresponding planes. Her native plane, however, lies beyond the three.

The physical plane itself is beset with terrible snares and difficulties. The astral or subtle plane is full of inconceivable temptations from which it is impossible for a jiva to escape unscathed.

Similarly, still greater glamor awaits a jiva in the causal plane. Again, it is no small adventure to enter spiritual planes by oneself alone. This path is strewn with thorns and is sharp as a razor's edge.

> *Strait is the gate, and narrow is the way which leadeth unto life, and few there be that find it.*
>
> MATTHEW 7:7

It is, therefore, all the more necessary that a seeker after Truth must first find an adept in Truth, fully conversant with the spiritual path leading to Reality, and obtain his lessons from him, and practice them under his direct supervision, guidance, and control. Without these prerequisites there cannot be a ghost of a chance for success. In Katha Upanishad, we come across a dictum:

*Awake, arise, and stop not until the Goal is
reached.*

The knowledge of God can be had from a man of God. At every step an aspirant feels the need of the Master's strong and long arm, which alone can reach him, save him, and keep him on the path and lead him correctly. Maulana Rumi says:

*First find a Pir (adept in the line) for without
a Pir the way is beset with dangers, difficulties, and tribulations.*

*Whoever attempts to walk on this path by himself is sure to be led astray by Satan and
thrown down the precipice.*

*Without the overpowering influence of a Godman you are bound to become bewildered by
the howling cries of ghouls.*

*Many a wise and intelligent person attempted
this path alone but by the wiles of the negative powers came to a sad end. Many a time
the ghouls imitate the sounds of the Master,
and these may drag thee to perdition.*

It is through the loving grace of the Master that a spirit can get out of the prison-house of the body. From here the Luminous Form of the Master directly takes charge of the spirit, and protects her at every step with his loving grace.

*The intricate and bewildering turns and twists
of the path are easily passed through with
the help of the Satguru.*

The subtle and causal planes are a vast wilderness for the soul, and it is unsafe for her to traverse them by herself. Maulana Rumi tells us in this context:

> *Take a fellow traveler with thee and travel not alone on this path. Do not venture in this wilderness by thyself alone.*

Hafiz Sahib also gives the same advice:

> *Do not attempt these stages alone. In the bewildering darkness, you are sure to lose your way.*

CHAPTER EIGHT

Without a Guru All is Darkness

WITHOUT A Guru we are in utter darkness. The Reality remains a mere miasma and a mirage. It is an unwritten law and unspoken language quite unintelligible except when a Master Soul by his personal attention makes it significant. The glamor of the world is so great and overbearing that passing phantoms appear stable and substantial, the untrue puts on the mantle of Truth, and we cannot possibly tear aside the magic veil and escape from the false charm in which we are enveloped. It is the Master's Grace that can pull a spirit out of the physical sheath right above the plane of senses, enabling her to move unfettered to higher spiritual visions and attain her native Godhead.

> *Without a Master, it is sheer darkness, and one sinks into bottomless depths.*

An embodied spirit cannot have bliss unless it obtains experience of itself through the grace of a living Master. He initiates her into esoteric knowledge, which has to be practiced in the laboratory of the human mind:

> *Without a Master there is blinding darkness, and one simply cannot know. Without a Master, spirit does not become Spirit, and there can be no salvation for her.*

> *Verily, verily, I say unto you that you must have a Master.*
> *O Mind! ye must turn to some Master Soul.*
> *Accept as Master an adept in the Sound Principle and he shall wash thee clean of all impurities.*
> *The Master both by his attention and his instruction imparts the Knowledge of Truth.*
> *He who has never seen a Master Soul nor accepted one, simply wastes his life in this world.*

A jiva is always in stark darkness. If he closes his eyes, there is darkness within. Again, he is enveloped in total ignorance. He who can dispel this darkness of jivas is called a Guru. The term *Guru* consists of two words: *Gu* meaning darkness and *Ru* meaning Light. Hence *Guru* means one who can lead us from darkness to Light, from untruth to Truth, and from death to Immortality. The illustrious poet, Kalidas, speaks of the Guru:

> *He converts darkness into Light and makes the invisible God visible.*

As a jiva is clothed in ignorance, all his actions too are born of ignorance and thus keep him in bondage.

The Saints declare that without a Master Soul to guide us, all charitable deeds and meritorious acts, like study of the scriptures, keeping of fasts and vigils, performance of pilgrimages, observance of social customs and rituals and scrupulous adherence to strict religious injunctions as of old, do not help in the liberation of a soul. Kabir Sahib, therefore, in very strong terms warns us against such acts:

> *The telling of beads and acts of charity, without a Master Soul to guide, go in vain.*

None of these bears any fruit. Bullah Shah tells us:

> *O Bullah! Without a Master all thy devotion would be barren.*

Unless the inner eye is opened and contact is established with the Power within, nothing can be of any avail. We have of necessity to seek a Master who is competent to wean us from all outer pursuits, pull the spirit out of the plane of the senses, and lead her step by step from one plane to another until she is led back to her pre-natal Home: *Sach Khand* or *Muqam-i-Haq*. He dispels all doubts born of darkness, and gives us Heaven's Light as a guide, unfailing and unfaltering.

> *With the Guru, the darkness is dispelled; Guru is there wherever one may turn.*

With no vision in our eyes, the light of hundreds of moons and thousands of suns can do us no good. Such a radiant effulgence would surely fail to end the darkness of the eyes. In exactly the same way, when there is no vision in the inner eye, we cannot see the wonderful brilliance of the soul, and we remain steeped in pitch darkness.

> *Hundreds of moons and thousands of suns together may rise;*
> *Even with such radiance, there is not a speck of Light.*

CHAPTER NINE

Historical Evidence

WE HAVE the testimony of history to show that one cannot have access to spiritual regions by one's own self. In the Shastras it is mentioned that Narad was refused admittance into Vishnupuri—The Land of Vishnu—when he by himself attempted to enter into that kingdom, because he had not been initiated by any Guru.

Again, Sukh Dev Swami, the son of Ved Vyas, with all his spiritual knowledge and learning, right from his conception in his mother's womb, could not enter the kingdom of Vishnu until he accepted Raj Rishi Janak as his spiritual mentor.

Nowhere do we come across any instance in which an uninitiated jiva by himself may have been allowed to enjoy this privilege.

All born Saints, though very few, come into the world with esoteric knowledge right from their birth but have for form's sake to adopt a Master.

Kabir Sahib, for instance, had to accept Shri Ramananda as his Master. In spite of their completed spiritual background, they had to associate with Saints, as one would do in a refresher course.

Guru Amar Das tells us that it is God's Law that one cannot even think of Him without being reminded of Him by some Master of Truth.

> *It is ordained by God Himself that one thinks of Him only when he meets a Master of Truth (Godman).*

Again:

> *No man can come to me except the Father which has sent me draw him; and I will raise him up at the last day.*
>
> JOHN 6:44

The generality of mankind simply cannot do without a Master Soul. Even Lord Rama and Lord Krishna, the very incarnations of Vishnu, had to bow down before Maharishi Vashisht and Ingris Rishi, respectively.

When such high-souled personages with sway extending as far as the causal region had to accept a Spiritual Guide, we ordinary human beings cannot dispense with this absolutely basic necessity.

Guru Nanak emphatically declares that the importance of *Guru* can be known from Brahma, Narad, and Ved Vyas:

> *O Brother! without a Guru, you cannot have absolute Truth (as opposed to relative knowledge through perception by the senses). You may verify this by reference to Brahma, Narad, and Vishnu.*

Tulsi Sahib says:

> *Who is greater than Rama and Krishna? They too, had to accept a Master. Lord of the three regions (physical, astral, and causal), they too, had to bow before a Master.*

Everyone who has made any mark in spirituality has had the backing of some Master Soul. Raj Rishi Janak got a practical demonstration in spirituality from Maharishi Ashtavakra. Gorakh Nath received his initiation from Machinder Nath. Arjuna, the warrior prince of the Pandavas, learned his lessons in spirituality from Lord Krishna. Swami Vivekananda sat at the feet of Paramhans Ramakrishna, the Saint of Dakhshineshwar.

Among the Sikhs, Guru Nanak molded Lehna and made Angad out of him (his *ang* or limb), and the latter, in turn, raised Amar Das to the status of a Guru, and so on.

Maulana Rumi tells us that he got his spiritual impetus from Shamas-i-Tabrez:

> *A maulvi (school teacher) could not become maulana (leader in theology),*
> *If it were not for the grace of Shamas-i-Tabrez.*

Again:
> *O Saqi (Master)! come and look with favor upon the Malauna;*
> *From housetops he cries: he is the slave of Shamas-i-Tabrez.*

Many a Mahatma has in his discourses paid homage to his divine preceptor, and though some have not made any such mention, there can be no denying the fact that Light comes from Light, and Life from Life, and that mind and matter-ridden jivas cannot awaken and arise in cosmic awareness unless pulled up by some Master Soul.

CHAPTER TEN

Before and After Guru Nanak

THERE IS always food for the hungry and water for the thirsty. A babe that was born five hundred years ago was provided by Dame Nature with milk from the mother's breast; and so was the case with one who came into the world a thousand years back. Those who are born in the present age are also being provided with similar means of sustenance.

The law of supply and demand is an immutable one in Nature. In exactly the same way this law works inexorably in spiritual matters also.

For the aspirants before the time of Guru Nanak or in this age or hereafter, Nature cannot but provide the means of satisfying their aspirations.

To delimit a particular period of one or two centuries as the period of Gurus and to say that there were no Master Souls before or after that particular time, is against the fundamental law of supply and demand, and hence incorrect.

The teachings of the Masters are for all times and not for any particular period. They utter eternal truths which hold good for eternity, and are the common heritage of mankind in general. Their seed-dictum for instance is that God is One and is the Gift of a Godman. It is an axiomatic truth, self-evident, and hardly needs any comment.

In *Anurag Sagar,* Kabir Sahib tells us that he came into the world in all the four yugas or cycles of time.

Bhagat Bani was in existence long before *Gurbani.* From *Guru Granth Sahib* and the verses of Bhai Gurdas, we learn that from age to age people benefited from Shabd or *Bani.*

> *Krishna and Balbhadra both bowed before a Guru.*
> *Namdev the calico printer and Kabir the weaver learned the esoteric science from a Guru.*
> *Bani has been in existence in all the four cycles of time and carries the message of Truth.*
> *Shabd is true, and Bani is true. Godmen have from age to age explained this.*

In the biography of Guru Nanak by Bhai Bala, Guru Nanak is said to have stated that in this *Kali Yuga* (Iron Age) many a Saint would come to lead people Godward.

> *Seventy Bhagats and fourteen Saints would come during this period.*
> *The Saints would carry shiploads of people Homeward. Those who would not believe would flounder, and those who are slaves of their lower selves would not be accepted.*

From the above it is clear that both Guru and *Gurbani* have always existed side by side. It is the Guru who has ever been the means of helping the seekers after Truth.

O God! Thy Saints have at all times been in the world.

O God! throughout the ages the line of Gurus has been in existence. The succession of Satgurus continues throughout and they have ever preached the lesson of Naam.

CHAPTER ELEVEN

Scriptures and Their Value

GURU IS A highly spiritual being with a sway extending as far as Sach Khand. He has a firsthand knowledge of And, Brahmand and Sach Khand: the three grand divisions from physical to purely spiritual realms.

Free from the clutches of body and mind, he is charged with pure spirituality. Unless a jiva comes into contact with such a being, his latent spiritual aspirations are not stirred up. The Guru is really a lighted candle that lights many blown-out candles. He can, by transmitting his own life impulse, enliven others. Some persons feel that by the study of scriptures alone they can have spiritual light and need no Master for this purpose. We may pause here and consider the value and worth of the sacred books or holy scriptures.

These are, after all, nothing but the records of the personal spiritual experiments and experiences of ancient sages, seers, prophets, and men of piety. It is good to read them with loving devotion. We should have respect for them, for they constitute a great treasure-house of spirituality which our forefathers have left for our benefit.

The sacred books and biographies of the high-souled personages create a spiritual longing and inspire us with hope and courage. We may to a certain extent become acquainted with the broad principles of spirituality, but cannot learn their right import nor get the life impulse, both of which come from a living Master alone.

Books are, after all, material things and matter cannot impart Life.

Life comes from Life as Light comes from Light. It is only an awakened soul that can rouse us from our deep slumber. We may read scriptures for ages upon ages and perform countless sacrificial deeds, but cannot have spiritual awakening and spiritual insight.

Spirituality can neither be bought nor taught, but may be caught like any infectious disease from one who may himself be spiritually infected, nay rather, obsessed.

The teachings of the Saints have not only to be learned but have also to be revealed. Besides knowledge of the theory of the Path, it has to be seen, experienced and verified. It is at once a science and an art, into the mysteries of which only an adept can safely lead, guide, and take us through.

> *God can best be served through devotion to a Godman, for it is by his grace that we can reach God.*

Again, even the scriptures and the past Masters emphatically exhort us to find a living Master.

> *Drink the washings of the Sadh's feet.*
> *Make a holocaust of thyself for his sake.*
> *Wash in the dust of his feet and be a sacrifice to him.*

> *Be ye a slave to the Saints—and this is all that ye need to know.*

Bhai Gurdas also tells us:

> *In the Guru lie hidden all the Vedas and the sacred scriptures. A contact with him is enough to help one to safely cross over the ocean of life. We cannot know Truth without the Master of Truth. God Himself has to come down for this very purpose.*

There are persons who studiously and scrupulously study the scriptures all their lives. They know a great deal by rote and can deliver learned discourses and give high-flown talks on spiritual matters, but unfortunately are altogether devoid of spiritual knowledge and spiritual experience. Their life and conduct is as blank as that of any other. They have not learned at the root nor drunk the Water of Life at the fountainhead of life: the living Master. In *Sri Asa Ki War*, we have:

> *One may stuff his head with so much learning and accumulate a heavy load of knowledge. He may raise and gather a regular harvest of learning. All his life he may go on studying from year to year, month to month, from moment to moment. O Nanak! One thing you may know for certain: he will become a bloated ass.*
>
> *O Nanak! One may study sacred lore by weight and be engaged ceaselessly in this*

> task. *What after all is the value of learning when Naam lies far beyond all holy books?*

Books, after all, contain a description of God's Knowledge, but cannot actually deliver the goods.

> *Know ye for certain that the essence of all knowledge and wisdom lies in Dhuni (Sound Principle) and as such it is indescribable.*

This essence then is within us, but we cannot have It unless we know how to tap inside, as Emerson puts it.

Dr. J. D. Rhine, the parapsychologist and researcher, tells us in his book *Mind and the New World* that there is something in man that transcends all matter. If spiritual knowledge could be had from books, then all the learned people would by now be saints.

But in actual experience we see that in spite of all their book learning they continue to be as material as the very libraries that house these books.

Laden with the dead weight of book knowledge, they may be likened to an ass staggering under the deadweight of sandalwood and experiencing not the sweet scent emanating therefrom.

Like a ladle in the pudding, they are ignorant of the taste of the pudding. In this age of learning, when the world is literally flooded with books, there is, unfortunately, no flood of spirituality and not even a sprinkling of spiritually-minded people.

It is only the advent of a Master of Truth that brings spirituality into the limelight and many there are who become dyed in spiritual colors. A conscious spirit can be activated and quickened into life by someone who is more conscious. Neither books nor intellectual knowledge can do this thing. No person, no matter how intellectual, can infuse Life in another unless he himself has Life.

To talk of spirituality is much easier than to live spiritually. Such persons only dabble in spirituality and just make a show of it, and cannot do any real good.

Maulana Rumi says:

> *Come under the overall influence of some Saint;*
> *Thou canst not find the path from a mere imitator.*

In the Gospel we find the words of Christ:

> *Beware of false prophets which come to you in sheep's clothing but inwardly they are ravening wolves.*
>
> MATTHEW 7:15

An association with a Saint is bound to create in a jiva a longing for spirituality. This, in fact, is the touchstone for the worldly-wise. Such a being is worthy of respect and adoration with all our hearts and souls. Whoever comes in contact with him is magnetized and is charged with spirituality and taken along to spiritual realms.

> *My body, mind, and wealth all belong to the Master;*
> *His Grace has provided the Holy Grail and made me whole;*
> *The world holds no greater benefactor than he,*

He who contacts a Sadh is ferried across safely.

The ideal of the Master is spiritual. He is not limited to his physical body as we are. He is Word personified.

The Word was made flesh and dwelt among us.

The physical body is just like a raiment which has to be cast off both by the disciple and the Master, the moment this spiritual journey begins; as it is the untrammeled spirit that has to tread the spiritual path. But so long as he works on the physical plane as a teacher to the stray brethren, blessed indeed is his form full of Godly Grace, shedding Godly Light around him and charging all and sundry with powerful rays of spirituality. Man is the teacher of man and ideal man has ever been the ideal of man.

Those who regard it as idolatry do not know the secret of the Master's greatness. This "man worship," as they call it, is much better than "book worship" or "idol worship," because it is a worship of Higher Consciousness by lower consciousness. Life can come from Life, not from inert matter. Hazrat Khusro, a great Sufi poet, in his well-known couplet, tells us:

People allege that Khusro has become an idol worshiper,
Verily do I admit it, for the world has nothing to do with me.

Again, another Persian poet from his sick bed said:

O ignorant physician! take thy leave, for thou

> *knowest not that for the love-sick there is no other remedy except the sight of his Beloved.*

Similarly, Guru Nanak in his childhood when afflicted with the pangs of love asked the physician who came to attend him to quit, as he could not find out the illness of his heart.

There is nothing in common between a worldly-wise man and a devotee. One who has never known devotion cannot know the worth of a Master, who is a polarized God, shedding kindly Light in the world.

Truly speaking, the term *Guru* is not an appellation of any person. It signifies and stands for a dynamic power that works in and through a particular human form and is the ideal for us all.

This is the power that helps in spiritual advancement. Like a floodlight he floods the world with his spiritual Light, and one cannot see anything besides Light. The aspirants for spirituality gather around him like moths and make a holocaust of themselves in his august and holy presence.

Kabir Sahib says:

> *The ignorant regard the Master as a human being and are caught in the whirlwind of the world and sink down. Their mind and body are of no consequence and they cannot gain anything. They cannot develop any devotion in themselves, hence cannot escape from bondage. Such jivas make a headlong dash for hell-fire, and ceaselessly move with the giant wheel of creation.*

CHAPTER TWELVE

Guru is Superman or Godman

AS A MAN, Guru is an ideal man: in him shines the very Sun of Spirituality. He is the fountainhead of Life. He is an epitome of the entire creation, visible and invisible, right from Sat Lok down to the physical plane. No one can know him fully, even as it is impossible to swim across an ocean. For a dip in the water one does not go into mid-ocean, but is content with the water at the beach or the bathing ghat. Through the perfect man one can enjoy the Love, Light and Life of God.

If we ask of his greatness, of his native place, how he has come down, and what his mission is in life, all that can be said is that he has come directly from the Kingdom of God or Sat Lok, and having crossed the various intermediary planes (*Tap Lok, Jan Lok, Swar Lok, Bhanwar Lok,* etc.) has reached the physical world or *Bhu Lok* just to manifest the Godhead that is his to the world-weary.

> *Come unto me, all ye that labor and are heavy laden, and I will give you rest.*
> MATTHEW 11:28

> *The Son of man is come to seek and to save that which was lost.*
> LUKE 19:10

Murshid-i-Kamil (Perfect Master) is a veritable abode of God's attributes in fullness and in abundance. The kindly Light of heaven shines in him and he diffuses it among mankind. The Love of God is surging in Him like heaving sea-waters.

> *The moving waters at their priest-like task of*
> *pure ablution, round earth's human shores.*
> KEATS

And, above all, he is the Life of Life, and his greatest mission is to impart the Life Impulse to the stark cold jivas all immersed in worldly pursuits, dead to higher instincts. God may well be perceived in Godman. It is said that God made man after His own image and asked the angels to bow before him. Maulana Rumi says:

> *He has placed the veritable sun in man.*

When a person rises in cosmic awareness, he finds that the Master is the hub of the entire universe. He is Truth personified, possessing the very essence of God and fit to be worshiped by all.

He is the leader and guide of mankind; the greatest, the highest and the perfect one among them. He is the genuine abode of all that is good and noble. He is the prototype of God, working as His viceroy and administering His laws on all planes (physical and spiritual). He is gifted with forensic acuteness, discriminative acumen and sound judgment. He may be unlettered, but still he is the most learned. Even as a man, he is the holiest of the holy, most pious and most loving; with love that far transcends societies, countries, and nations. His self is co-eval with mankind. He is the citizen of the world, and his appeal is one of universal interest. He is, in short, the deputy of God, come into the world to share His Love, Light, and Life with erring humanity.

In this world, he lives just like any other individual. Although in the world, he is not of the world. He loves all people much more than parents love their children. He knows but looks beyond our shortcomings and smilingly helps us to overcome them. Full of compassion, Christ-like, with sore and bruised feet, the Son of Man ceaselessly goes about with insatiable hunger in his soul, passionately seeking to recover and retrieve that which is lost: lost man, his brother, lost soul.

He may look like a man, but in reality he is more than a man, more than a Superman, indeed. He is perfect in every respect: physically, mentally, morally, spiritually, and as a manifestation of God. With all his greatness, he works as the lowliest of the low and humblest of the humble. He combines in himself power and poverty, intellect and love, greatness and humility.

Master of Truth as he is, he far excels even a Superman. His sway extends to purely spiritual regions, which lie beyond human limitations of time, space, and causation. He can at will leave the physical body, tread the sun and moon, traverse subtle and causal planes, and transcend Par Brahm and beyond.

Science with its material accomplishments is groping in the dark. All scientific research is still in the material world where the scientists are relentlessly working with all the mental and moral force at their command. They have no idea of the various planes to which the Master of Truth has access at his free will and sweet pleasure.

Those who accept the Master's teachings and work under his direction can see for themselves. All the Saints are at one in their conclusion:

The Kingdom of God lies within.

Christ tells us:

The Kingdom of God cometh not with observation; neither shall they say, Lo here! or, lo there! for, behold, the Kingdom of God is within you.
LUKE 17:20-21

Again, in *Gurbani,* we have:

Everything is within you and nothing is outside you. Quest without is fruitless, when the crest jewel, O brethren, is lodged within you.
He who searches without is yet in the wilderness.

The human body is the Temple of God. It is the real church, the synagogue, and the mosque made by God, and what a pity we try to seek Him in man-made houses. One who knows how to cut deep in the cavern of the mind and experiment in the laboratory of the soul can successfully see the wonder of sublime sights and hear the celestial strains of the harmony divine.

In the body lies everything: Khand, Mandal

and Patal (inner planes, high and low, including the nether world). In it is lodged the crest jewel of spirituality, and a devotee can have this in abundance. The entire macrocosm is in the microcosm. In this body one can find Naam (Word) if one were to follow the instructions of the Master.

Sannai, the great philosopher, tells us:

In the kingdom of the human body there are innumerable firmaments and powers that work in order. The spirit has to traverse many a high and low region, mountain and river valley. There are many plains, oceans, wildernesses and bewildering heights of which one can hardly conceive. In this mighty maze the physical world is just like a tiny speck on a big ocean.

The human body, being the Temple of God, is just a model of the grand creation and whoever delves into it is able to know the secret of the creation.

Brahmand and Pind have been fashioned alike. The investigations of the one automatically reveal the mystery of the other, like an open book.

Great indeed is man, gifted as he is with untold possibilities. The very macrocosm is lodged in the microcosm of the body. We, however, look to outer raiment and are concerned with it constantly, little knowing what is behind the folds of this garment. We nourish and pamper the body but allow the roots to run dry. The roots of the entire creation originate in the subtle region, which we can reach by a process of inversion.

> *Verily I say unto you, whosoever shall not receive the Kingdom of God as a little child, he shall not enter therein.*
>
> MARK 10:15

But, unfortunately, we never have a peep within, because we are averse to becoming as a little child. Emerson, a great philosopher, also exhorts us to *tap inside*. Bergson advises us to take a *mortal leap within* to land at the source of all knowledge.

The lessons of the process of inversion, tapping inside, the mortal leap within, or becoming as a little child, as Jesus puts it, are given in detail by the Master of Truth, both by word of mouth and by instructions on the various planes as the spirit travels onward under his personal guidance and care.

Saints are scientists of the spiritual world and Masters of *Para Vidya*—Knowledge of the Beyond; i.e., knowledge of that which lies beyond reason and intellect and can be learned or known through the sense of perception.

It is a subject of extra-sensory perception (ESP) as it is called by the modern psychic science researchers and parapsychologists, who, as Dr. J. D. Rhine tells us in his book *Mind and the New World,* have discovered through their investigations that there is something operative in the human being which transcends the laws of matter.

The Master of Truth is fully conversant with that *something,* and is competent to grant the full extra-sensory perception, as an eye-surgeon can restore sight to the physical eyes. The Master, like Buddha, tells us that physical life is all misery, but that beyond it there are countless subtle planes where one experiences nothing but bliss and light. Every day, he goes to these planes and tells us of his experiences. Those who follow his instructions and experiment in the laboratory of the mind under his guidance, see subtle worlds just as we see the physical, and the results are as sure, certain and definite as two and two make four.

CHAPTER THIRTEEN

Master and the Homegoing of Jivas

MASTER comes from his spiritual abode to call the jivas back home.

> *No man can come to me, except the Father which hath sent me draw him.*
> JOHN 6:44

Our spirit is exactly of the same essence as God's. Having been separated from that ocean of bliss it has become imprisoned in the prison-house of body and mind. Saints also come down from their spiritual abode to take back home such spirits as are prepared for the return journey.

It is, in fact, God Himself who comes in the garb of man to lead the jivas out of the tentacles of the Negative Powers, after they have served the period of probation. This is the fulfillment of the grand covenant or the great law—Man is to be the teacher of man—teaching the true redemption, and home-going with rejoicing.

> *When the dead shall hear the Voice of the Son of God . . . they that hear shall live.*
> JOHN 5:25

> *He who sent thee into the world calls thee back. Return ye to thy native home in Sahaj (beyond the three-fold regions, physical, mental, and causal).*

One with God, they come into this world under His behest as His plenipotentiaries to administer His law concerned with home-going. This is their noble mission, and gracefully they fulfill His purpose. Shamas-i-Tabrez tells us about himself:

> *Little can you imagine what type of birds we are, and what we keep warbling all the time. We may look to be a beggar, but our actions are more than kingly. We may appear to be poor, but we are richer than the richest mine. When we are king of kings we care not for the brief stay in this prison-house of the world. We are just a pilgrim here, and cannot remain for long. We hold a covenant with the Lord and stand true to our troth. So long as we are in physical raiment we do not get annoyed with anybody nor do we vex another. Like a veritable paradise we are ever filled with kindly light and heavenly grace. Happily do we live with a cheery heart and a smile on our lips.*

Guru Gobind Singh likewise tells us of himself:

> *Casting off the duality, I had become one with the Lord. Never did I like to come down again into the world, but it was at His bidding that I had to yield, and I came to fulfill His purpose.*

Kabir Sahib also says:

> *Kabir comes from the celestial abode of the*

> Lord and holds a direct commission (*instrument of instruction*) *from Him.*

Again, in the Gospel, we have:

> *I do nothing of myself; but as my Father hath taught me, I speak these things.*
>
> JOHN 8:28

In *Gurbani,* we also come across similar references:

> *O Lalo! I speak nothing from myself. I simply utter what the Beloved puts into my mouth.*

> *Poor Nanak opens his mouth only when he is bidden to do so.*

CHAPTER FOURTEEN

Master and His Mission

MASTER SOULS come into the world out of sheer compassion for suffering humanity.

> *Come unto me, all ye that labour and are heavy laden, and I will give you rest.*
> MATTHEW 11:28

They have of necessity to put on the physical raiment, full of impurity as it is, because they have to work on the physical plane among human beings.

> *God clothed Himself in vile man's flesh, that so He might be weak enough to suffer woe.*
> JOHN DONNE

The way in which they come into and go out of the world is, however, quite different from ours. They come and go of their own free will; while we do so under the irresistible force of karmic pressure, just as a prisoner would enter a prison under a sentence of penal servitude. They come for the benefit of mankind—to grant the Life Impulse to such embodied souls as yearn for Life. Disembodied and eternally free, they come as Saviours of souls.

> *They that are whole have no need of the physi-*

> cian, but they that are sick. I came not to call the righteous, but sinners to repentance.
>
> MARK 2:17

> Birth and death affect them not, for they come as Saviours for the sinners. By transmitting their own life energy, they transform the disciples into Saints.

A Master Soul is the greatest benefactor on earth. His work is of the highest order. He comes to liberate the souls from the vast prison-house of mind and matter, so that he may take the exiles back to their glorious home and restore them to their rich heritage. A kindly soul may direct the prison warden to provide delicious food for the prisoners under his charge. Another may grant the boon of delicacies to them. A third may order for them good clothing and lodging and so on. Each of them no doubt may do something to ameliorate their lot for the time being.

But if someone were to throw open the prison gate and ask them to escape the squalor and misery of the jail, his work would naturally be counted as one far excelling the works of others.

This is exactly the nature of the work of a Master Soul. He reveals to us the Lost Kingdom, and restores us to Paradise from which Adam and, through him, his progeny were driven out for the original disobedience to God's Commandment.

Man had an ignoble fall from the Garden of Eden, and none could restore him to the good grace of the

Father and bring about reconciliation except the Son of Man. He takes upon himself the vicarious responsibility for the sins of man, purifies him of all ignominy and by a transfusion of his own Life Impulse makes him arise into cosmic awareness and gain everlasting life.

He that believeth on the Son hath everlasting life.

JOHN 3:36

CHAPTER FIFTEEN

Master and His Work

MASTER is like a wish-yielding tree. He always grants the wishes, whatever they are, of the seekers. The rich and the poor, the high and the low: everyone comes to him for something. His greatest pleasure, however, lies in liberating spirits from the clutches of body and mind. Irrespective of his denominational character, he attends to the spiritual needs of all.

He neither creates new "isms" nor does he denounce the "isms" in existence. He comes not to break the law, but to fulfill the law. All "isms" (spiritual), in fact, receive strength and solidarity from him.

In his inimitable loving way, he takes everyone from the line of least resistance. He does not interfere with the creeds and beliefs of a person, whatever these are, nor does he meddle with the social order of things. He simply talks of the spirit, its intrinsic nature, its seat in the body, its various operative processes, its latent capabilities, and how it can be developed in its relation with body, mind, and with God, and how it can be liberated, made self-poised and turned Godward.

His appeal is directly to spirit, and his words sink deep into the very depths of the soul. He deals with ready cash at the counter and does not make people live in hope till the end of their lives or thereafter. He teaches:

Believe not the words of a Master. Soul unless you see the things he tells about with your own eyes.

It is just for the sake of experiment that we have in the first instance to accept the words of a Master. But when we find the truth of what he says, by actual experimentation, then the hypothesis is turned into conviction.

When a person once sees the light of the sun, he cannot deny the existence of the sun even though the bats of the world may unite in denying the solar phenomenon.

Unless the inner vision is approached, the Truth of the Reality does not dawn, and the jivas or embodied spirits remain groping in utter darkness and ignorance of the highest and the greatest magnitude.

Whenever a Master of Truth comes into the world, the spiritually hungry and thirsty gather around him and quench their hunger and thirst by the manna and the Elixir of Life that he freely gives to the aspirants.

Gradually their love develops into a steady devotion that befits them more and more for the saving grace of the Master, and helps a jiva to travel quickly home.

CHAPTER SIXTEEN

Master and His Duties

COUNTLESS are the duties and responsibilities of a Master. His first and foremost work is to link once again the created with the Creator; to win for him the Kingdom of God and restore him to his ancient and forgotten lineage and heritage. This he does by means of Shabd or Word, which carries the spirit to its native Home.

Like electromagnetic waves, the Shabd or Word is vibrating everywhere, but, unfortunately, through the overpowering density and weight of matter on the physical plane we are unable to feel it and harness it to our benefit.

A Master, by his personal guidance, frees the spirit from the dead weight of matter, disengages it from the sensory organs, withdraws its everspreading rays and collects them at its center, behind the two eyebrows, thereby enabling it to experience a little of the Light of God and to hear Shabd, the Voice of God; both of which by continuing practice can be developed in course of time.

The jiva then finds himself attracted by that magnetic power, the Sound Principle, which carries him step by step to his ultimate goal. A mere knowledge of the science of the Masters cannot be of any avail, and intellectualism by itself, however keen, cannot be of any aid.

An ethical life is a stepping stone to spirituality. Cleanliness is said to be next to Godliness. A Master, therefore, begins his work with man-making. Cleanliness in thought, word and deed is an essential which cannot be over-emphasized. As self-knowledge precedes God-Knowledge, a Master has first to impart in theory and practice the knowledge of the spirit, to liberate it from the shackles of mind and body.

Gradually the spirit is enabled to cast off the various coverings or sheaths with which it is enshrouded, until it becomes spirit clean, untrammeled and unalloyed, and exultantly cries out, "I am Spirit!"

After this comes training in God-Knowledge, which is the climax and the crest jewel in the science of spirituality, and enables the spirit to attain Godhead.

Once the shepherd takes charge of a lost sheep and brings it to his fold, he takes over the entire responsibility. Once a Master, always a Master, is a well-known dictum. Master on earth, he is Master in the various regions, subtle, causal, and beyond. He does not rest until a spirit is safely escorted back to the Father's mansion in Heaven.

The process of home-going and progress on the path is entirely at his discretion, and he is the sole judge for the time and measure of each step Godward.

From the time the spirit crosses over to the astral plane and comes face to face with the self-luminous form of the Master, the jiva has nothing more to do and strive for. It is the Master's job henceforth.

Apart from this a Master is a child of Light, and like a lighthouse over tempestuous seas sheds his kindly Light throughout the world. Like the good shepherd he has to look after and tend many sheep. Whoever has anything to do with a Master Soul is ultimately to be prepared for the path and helped through in his probation and apprenticeship.

CHAPTER SEVENTEEN

Guru is Godman

MASTER is in truth the perfect manifestation of God. Filled with Godly Light he is the torch-bearer of God. He is the pole from which God works out His plan of redemption. God, having made man after His own image, placed an iron wall between Himself and the spirit, owing to the first sin of disobedience to Him. Man was thus driven out from the Garden of Eden and placed in the physical world, so the story goes, to earn his bread with the sweat of his brow, and to work out his salvation through a Saviour—the Son of Man, in which garb God Himself comes with the key to unlock the Kingdom of Heaven for leading in the lost sheep.

The Word becomes flesh and dwells among us, God's Light shines through his eyes, God's voice speaks through him, and God's Grace works out salvation for those who hunger and thirst for Him. Like a common man, he lives among us, shares our joys and sorrows, gives us instructions in spirituality and guides us on the path. Embedded in the Father he works out His Will.

All things are delivered unto me of my Father: and no man knoweth the Son, but the Father; neither knoweth any man the Father,

> *save the Son, and he to whomsoever the Son will reveal Him.*
>
> MATTHEW 11:27

Maulana Rumi also says:

> *In the Master is lodged both God and the Mediator. There is in fact not the least distinction between the two. Drive all thought of duality from thy mind, or else thou shalt get lost in the wilderness, and so also shall be the fate of thy first lessons in spirituality. He who considers the two as separate entities has not yet learnt anything from, or known anything of, the Master.*

Master is the form of the formless God—the form that we can see and have relationship with. It is this very form that imparts to us the knowledge of God, and again it is this very form, luminous of course, that accompanies us on the journey Godward and directs our footsteps on the path.

In each plane, physical, causal, and beyond, there is increased splendor of the Master, and his limitless sway and power becomes more manifest to the companion spirit as it travels along.

Godman as he is, in the world his form is the *Kibla* and *Kaaba* of the Muslims, the altar of the Christians, the eternal light of the Zoroastrians, the temple, the synagogue and the *Gurdwara,* for he alone is fit to be worshiped.

Like electricity in the atmosphere, the universe is

charged through and through with God. There is no place where He is not, and yet He is hidden from view; and Guru or Master is the mighty switch, the source and fountainhead that makes it possible for us to witness His greatness and get glimpses of His power.

In short, Master is the pole at which God actually works, and therefore he may fittingly be called *polarized* God as distinguished from the latent state in which He is at one with everything and yet we know Him not.

The greatness and the puissance of God is manifested in the Master in abundance. So long as a person does not come in contact with some Godman, God just remains an idea with him, a mere figment of his everyday mind, a shadow with no real substance at all.

In the Godman, one finds a living God on earth, just as anyone talking and smiling with us, guiding us by word and example and helping us through from stage to stage. Blessed indeed is a spirit that can establish a living contact with a living Master—the greatest gift of God to mankind.

Man indeed is the teacher of man. Unless a Godman gives us Light, we cannot have the Light of Reality, and like blind men we grope in utter darkness.

In the physical world we, with physical eyes, can see nothing but physicality around us. The subtle vision can see the subtle world, and the causal can view the causal universe. Master of all three and even beyond, he bestows inner Light that illumines the inner darkness and one begins to witness an endless panorama of spiritual vistas ever expanding and bringing to view new delights at every step. All this work he does by means of the Sound Current or the Voice of God, hearing which the dead are quickened with Life and attain life everlasting. He is the connecting link between a soul and the Oversoul. With roots embedded in God and branches spreading throughout the world, laden with flowers and fruits of Paradise, he provides spiritual food to all who come to him.

Maulana Rumi in this context says:

> *O Friend! sit near one who knows the condition of thy heart (and who can make it whole). Rest a while under the shade of a tree that is laden with fresh and fragrant flowers. Loiter not in the market place from shop to shop, as idlers do. Go straight to one who has a store of honey with him.*
>
> *Take hold of the garment, O brave soul! of one who knows well the various planes: physical, mental, supramental, and beyond; and is able to remain with thee like a true friend, whether in life or in death, in this world or in the next.*

The form, physical or astral, of the Master or God-in-man which helps us through in our journey Godward, is better by far than the native invisible form of God which is beyond all thought and contemplation.

Brahma, Vishnu, Shiva, Ishwar (Niranjan) and Parmeshwar (incarnations of Brahma) are all worthy of our respect and adoration.

We have read much about them, religiously, in sacred lore. They figure as heroes and heroines in mythological tales, but as such are nothing but figments of human imagination.

When *Satguru* or the Master of Truth takes charge of a spirit (at *Gaggan*), He gradually reveals the true significance and way of each of them. All of them have existed since creation, and are engaged in carrying on the duties assigned to each of them.

But we cannot know them or their handiwork and authority unless the Satguru takes us along and shows us the nature of this mysterious hierarchy.

God Himself in the garb of man (Saints and prophets) informs us of His Own Natural Self. Guru Amar Das has therefore declared:

It is the basic principle of God that without a Master of Truth, no one can even think of Him.

Sant Kabir also tells us:

The Master is greater than God. Ye may very well think over this dictum. Devotion to God keeps a person entangled on this side (in the physical plane); but devotion to the Guru leads him across to God.

The greatness of the Master lies in this: that he connects the souls with the Unknown Reality, and puts a stop to the cycle of births and deaths. The Oversoul, even when with us, could neither manifest Itself directly nor could It take the soul out of the physical plane and liberate it.

Only through instructions from a Guru (Master Soul or Godman) and association with Shabd (Word or God-in-Action) can one achieve these wondrous results.

> *Without Word one can have no escape (from bondage).*
> *Word Personified is the Master and he can manifest It in us.*
> *God may turn His back and one may not mind, but if the Master does so, none can bring about reconciliation.*
>
> KABIR
>
> *If Siva gets estranged, the Master can reconcile us to him; but who can reconcile us to the Master?*

In this respect Sehjo Bai, a lady devotee, sings to us in melodious strains of the greatness of her Master—Charan Das:

> *I may give up God, but cannot for a moment forget the Master, for God Himself cannot come up to him.*
> *God drove me into the wilderness of the world, but the Master has snapped for me the ceaseless cycle of transmigration.*
> *God set on my heels the five deadly sins (desire, anger, greed, infatuation, and egoism), but the Master taking pity on my helplessness saves me from them.*
> *God entangled me in the meshes of the family ties, but the Master cut asunder these bonds.*

God delivered me to disease, decay and death, but the Master with his yogic powers delivered me from them.

God bound me hand and foot in the web of karmic reactions, but the Master revealed to me my true nature—and I have now found out that I am soul, the spirit of the universe.

God in me hid Himself behind a curtain, but the Master with his torch of Truth revealed God to me.

Again God created both bondage and salvation, but the Master put an end to all these chimerical fantasies.

I would sacrifice my very body and soul for Charan Das, my Master. I would rather surrender God for the Master's sake.

CHAPTER EIGHTEEN

Gurudev

(The Astral or Self-Luminous Form of the Master)

THE TERM *Dev* is derived from the Sanskrit root *Div* meaning "Light." The words *Guru Dev* are therefore used to denote the astral or luminous form of the Master as he appears in astral regions, after leaving the physical plane to guide the spirit as it transcends the physical body.

Theosophical literature refers to the luster of Master Souls in subtle and causal planes extending for miles and miles. Tulsi Sahib likewise tells us that the nails of the Guru's feet shine like *Mani* (a crest jewel in the head of a toad that shines forth like a flashlight in darkness). This astral light bestows vision to the third eye.

> *Blinding Light flashes forth from the nails of the Master's Feet and illumines the very soul of the devotee.*

Maulana Rumi speaks of It:

> *As the Light of the Master dawns in the soul, one gets to know the secrets of both worlds.*

A real Guru is the true manifestation of God. He is, in fact, Satguru or Master of Truth, and manifests in the world the Light of Truth.

> *O Nanak! Guru is the Satguru; I would like to touch the Feet of the Satguru.*

The term *Guru Dev,* therefore, signifies the self-luminous form of the Master, which is free from and far above his physical body, and which the spirit actually perceives with its inner subtle Light. When the spirit comes face to face with the astral Master, all doubts vanish and its labors get the crowning reward—the *summum bonum* of life.

> *Guru Dev gives vision to the eyes. All doubts become airy nothings and love's labor receives its crowning glory.*

Jesus Christ in the Gospel speaks thus:

> *If therefore thine eye be single, thy whole body shall be full of light.*
>
> MATTHEW 6:22

Guru Arjan tells us that the Blessed Form of the Master manifests itself in the forehead of a devotee.

> *The Blessed Form of the Master is in my forehead. Whenever I peep within I see him there.*

A Muslim Divine also speaks like this:

> *The image of the Beloved is in the mirror of my very heart. I see him with just a little turn of the head downward.*

It is this astral or self-luminous form of the Master that

leads a spirit Godward through various planes intervening between the physical plane and *Sat Lok* or the Region of Truth. There is no distinction between Guru and Guru Dev and Satguru and God.

It is one and the same current of divine compassion that assumes different names at different regions.

Following the law of similitude, the Divine Current as It materializes on the physical plane for the benefit of the aspirants is called *Guru* or Master, who by word of mouth imparts the spiritual instructions as any other teacher would do.

As the spirit of an aspirant leaves the body and is ready for the journey in the astral or subtle planes, that very Divine Current assumes a subtle form for the soul's benefit and guidance.

This subtle form disengaged from the bodily form of the Guru is termed *Guru Dev*. It is self-luminous and lustrous with Light extending over miles and miles. *Satguru* or the Master of Truth is the Power of Truth or God that works through both Guru and Guru Dev. With roots firmly embedded in *Sat* or Truth, he directly derives his inspiration from the eternal and unchangeable permanence, *Sat,* hence is known as *Satguru.*

Thus we see how the *Sat Dhara* or the current from *Sat* flows down, creating regions upon regions far below, ending with the physical plane.

It is this very current that also helps in taking the jivas back home, and is differently known as *Guru, Guru Dev* and *Satguru,* at different places, until the very roots of *Sat* are reached, and here the spirit cries out in wonder *Wah-i-Guru*, which means, "What a glory is thine, O Guru!"

Indescribable and beyond comprehension! So we have in Gurbani:

> *Guru Dev is Satguru, Par Brahm, and Parmeshwar. O Nanak! a Salutation to Guru Dev is Salutation to Hari or God.*

This very *Sat* or Truth is at one with the Guru as he works on the physical plane. Hence, it is said:

> *Blessed is the physical form of the Master, filled as it is to the brim with full power from above.*

> *The Greatness of the Master is indescribable and beyond all comprehension, for he is Par Brahm, Parmeshwar, beyond perception and knowledge.*

> *Guru Dev can neither be known nor measured. By following the instructions one can penetrate far into the mysteries of the past, the present, and the future. It is through his sheer Grace that one begins to know something of the unknown and the unknowable.*

In the physical world he works and acts like a Guru or Master; but when a jiva after some spiritual practice and discipline is ready to leave the *Pind* or body and is about to enter *And* (the subtle plane), the Guru comes to his aid in subtle shining form as his Guru Dev. Here he works as a connecting link between Guru and Satguru for he takes over the charge of a spirit from the Guru in the body, and leads her across to Satguru and Sat Purush.

Guru Dev meets and greets the spirit as it crosses the border lying between the physical and subtle regions by passing through the stars, the sun and the moon, spoken of in the *Vedas* as *Devian* and *Pitrian Margs* (Paths). This astral form is exactly like the physical form of the Master, but much more beautiful, luminous, and magnetic.

Maulana Rumi tells us:

> *Should you desire to see this refulgent Light, turn homeward like Ibrahim. Pass through the big star and the sky and the blue beyond. Steadily walk over the sun and the moon, and then you will find yourself in the heavenly Presence.*

Guru Nanak refers to this illuminated path, thus:

> *The Luminous Form of the Master is wondrously enrapturing and enchanting. Only a perfect Master can manifest this to a spirit.*

This lustrous form of the Master always accompanies a spirit in the various planes, ending with *Sach Khand* or the Home of Truth. When his luminous form descends to the focus of the eyes, a devotee has nothing more to strive for. Herein lies the devotion of the devotee. Half his success has been achieved, and hereafter the Master's astral form takes over the charge of the spirit with full responsibility for leading it to the final goal. Even the Saints also adore this form and derive ecstatic delight from it.

> *The Blessed Feet of the Beloved Guru Dev are worshiped by the Saints, the beloved of God.*

Khwaja Moeen-ud-Din Chisti also talks of the Luminous Form of the Master:

> *O Master! The sun cannot stand the resplendence of Thy Face.*
> *The moon also has covered herself with clouds to escape Thy Dazzling Light.*
> *The sun having borrowed his brilliance from the dust of Thy Feet has pitched his golden pavilion on the blue sky. If a single ray of Thy Face were to shoot forth into the sky, the sun would in shame go behind a veil. In the very Person of the Nabi (Prophet), the Light of God has taken up a material form just as the light of the sun does in the body of the moon.*

Maulana Rumi also refers to the lustrous form of his Master thus:

> *What dost thou know of the King of Kings that keeps me company?*
> *Cast thou a glance within me and be not deceived by my outer appearance.*

St. John has similarly described in the Bible his experience with the Luminous Form within:

> *I was in the Spirit . . . and heard behind me a great voice, as of a trumpet, . . .*
>
> *And I turned to see the voice that spake with me. And being turned, I saw . . . one like unto the Son of man, clothed with a garment down to the foot, and girt about the paps with a golden girdle.*
>
> *His head and hairs were white like wool, as white as snow; and his eyes were as a flame of fire;*
>
> *And his feet were like unto fine brass, as if they burned in a furnace; and his voice as the sound of many waters. . . .*
>
> *And his countenance was as the sun shineth in his strength.*
>
> REVELATION 1:10, 12-16
>
> *After this I looked, and, behold, a door was opened in heaven: and the first voice which I heard was as it were of a trumpet talking with me; which said, Come up hither, and I will show thee things which must be hereafter.*
>
> REVELATION 4:1

In the *Sar Bachan* of Swami Ji Maharaj, we have a similar reference:

> *Wondrous strange was the Form; No words could this Glory write.*

Hafiz, a mystical poet of great reknown, tells us:

> *Like the newborn moon the pure of sight may see;*
> *His Glory would not manifest to every eye.*

The astral form of the Master Soul is unchangeable and permanent. It is the form that guides aspirants to their goal.

> *Guru Dev is in the beginning of creation. He is in the beginning of each age and continues from age to age. Through Guru Dev alone can one reach Hari.*

Guru Arjan speaks of Guru Dev:

> *Salutations to Guru Eternal (Har Rai);*
> *Salutations to Guru of the Age (Sat Purush or Ram Rai);*
> *Salutations to Satguru (the manifestation of Sat Purush); and*
> *Salutations to Guru Dev (the Refulgent and Self-Luminous Form of the Guru, the connecting link between Guru and Satguru, responsible for guiding and leading a spirit through various planes).*

Guru Dev is the greatest and highest manifestation of Sat Purush. He is the controlling power of God and can grant salvation. By devotion to him one gets all comfort.

Nothing but *Sat* is Guru Dev; false is all worship apart from his.

Guru Arjan in his memorable words sings of the greatness of Guru Dev thus:

> *Gurudeva is father; Gurudeva is mother; and he is the Master and God Himself;*
> *Gurudeva is a real friend; dispeller of dark ignorance and breaker of all ties;*
> *Gurudeva is the bestower of Naam, an incantation of which chases away all evils;*
> *Gurudeva is the embodiment of peace, truth and intelligence, and truly a philosopher's stone;*
> *Gurudeva is a place of pilgrimage, fountain of the Elixir of Life, and light of reason;*
> *Gurudeva ordains everything, destroys sins and purifies the sinners;*
> *Gurudeva is ever eternal from the creation and beginning of each age, and his Word has a saving Grace;*
> *Gurudeva is the greatest gift of God, which, if granted, saves the worst sinners;*
> *Gurudeva is Satguru, Par Brahm, and Parmeshwar.*
> *Salutations to him, O Nanak.*

Gurbani tells of the immense benefit that one enjoys on meeting Guru Dev:

The five deadly sins—desire, anger, greed, infatuation, and egoism—just vanish.

Myriads of Karmic impressions of countless ages are destroyed. He pulls a jiva from body and mind consciousness and ushers it into cosmic awareness, where it no longer experiences the fires of the world in which the entire humanity is trapped.

Even in the world all the soul's desires are fulfilled. His course is soft and smooth thereafter, and receives acclamations from every side.

In this *Kali Yuga* (Iron Age) of iniquity and darkness Guru Dev serves as a beacon light on the stormy sea of life, and safely pilots sinners to the Heaven of peace and bliss. A saved soul in its turn pulls along all who are near and dear to it.

The manifestation of Guru Dev depends purely on the grace of God and one's special merits in one's progress on the spiritual path.

CHAPTER NINETEEN

Perfect Master
(Murshid-i-Kamil)

IN ORDER to derive full benefit from *Para Vidya* (Science of Spirituality), it is absolutely necessary to have the guidance of a living Master, or an adept both in the science and art of spirituality. He must be a *Murshid-i-Kamil* or perfect Saint who can lead aspirants to perfection. *If the blind leads the blind, both fall into a ditch* is a common aphorism too well known to need any comment.

There are various grades and stages on the spiritual path. A Saint of the highest order alone can safely take the jivas to the pinnacle of spirituality. One who is a novice or has climbed half-way cannot take a jiva to the top.

In an educational institution we see that there are different types of teachers for different classes. In this science also there a number of grades and degrees, as for instance, *Sadh, Sant, and Param Sant.*

For a proper understanding of the theory and practice of spirituality, we need the help of at least a *Sant* or Saint. A *Sadh* (one who has successfully transcended the physical, astral, and causal planes, and is above body and mind consciousness) can give us a lead, and befit us for further training from a Saint; but one who is not yet a Sadh cannot be of any help. For complete liberation from the cycle of birth and death, a Master Saint is necessary.

A perfect Master has no hallmark on his person. It is by personal contacts that one gradually begins to know something of his greatness, just as a student when he advances in studies gets to know little by little something of the ability of his teacher.

Again, the Master cannot disclose all his greatness at once, but only in proportion as an aspirant shows his keenness and makes progress on the path. The Master starts just like an ordinary teacher and imparts instructions as any friend or well-wisher would do. In course of time, he demonstrates the authority of a *Murshid* or Master on the path, and finally is seen embedded in *Sat* or Truth as *Satguru* or the Master of Truth; until there comes a stage when he and God appear merged in each other with no line of demarcation between them.

CHAPTER TWENTY

How to Find a Perfect Master and Know Him

To FIND A perfect Master is not so easy as it may seem. While living on the plane of the senses all the time, we have not the eyes with which to recognize the human pole from which the power of God works in the world. Yet where there is a will, there is a way. All that is required of an aspirant is the sincerity of purpose, intense longing and a burning passion for the Lord above everything else. Where there is fire, oxygen of itself comes to its aid. The principle of demand and supply works equally alike in all the spheres of life from the physical to the spiritual. There is always food for the hungry and water for the thirsty.

> *Ask and it shall be given unto you; seek and ye shall find; knock, and it shall be opened unto you.*
> MATTHEW 7:7

> *No man can serve two masters: for either he will hate the one, and love the other; or else he will hold to the one, and despise the other. Ye cannot serve God and mammon.*
> MATTHEW 6:24

For in the Bible we have:

> *I the* LORD *thy God am a jealous God . . .*

And in the same way Godman, like God, demands from his lovers an exclusive and unstinted love unto himself and unless one is prepared to sacrifice his all—body, mind, possessions—the way unto Him is not opened; nor can we come near to the Godman who makes manifest the way.

When the chela is ready, the Guru appears is the Law of God. How can a blindfolded person reach the ringmaster's cell by himself?

> *No man can come to me, except the Father which hath sent me draw him.*
> JOHN 6:44

Those whom God wills are of themselves drawn to the Godman, or the Godman himself finds them out, no matter where they may be.

Similarly, to know the Godman in his fullness is not given to man. We can have only such glimpses of his greatness as he may choose to grant. He alone is the judge of the time and measure of each advance and reveals to us gradually as much of his spiritual wealth as he wishes, and this he does by degrees as he qualifies us to grasp and understand and to hold it safely in trust. As one proceeds along in his company on the inner spiritual path, one gets to know him more and more as he sees his power working in all the inner planes from end to end until in the purely spiritual region (Muqam-i-Haq or Sach Khand), he appears in his Primal Manifestation (*Ek-Ankar*). On the physical plane, he is Word made flesh and dwells among us according to the laws of the earth-plane, and like any other worldly teacher, he teaches us; not, of course, of this world, but of a world totally different from this, a world that is self-luminous and is studded with stars, moons and suns in countless numbers. While apparently sharing with us our joys and sorrows of the world, he yet remains far above the pairs of opposites, endlessly imparts to us his spiritual instructions, both without and within, encouraging us at every step by his words of wisdom and in countless diverse ways inspires in us the Love of God and exhorts us to glorify Him.

Though ever kind the Master is, yet none can claim his grace; his grace flows alike to all, yet each gets his fill as he ordains.

Satguru is Sat Personified and knows one and all; himself in all, yet he remains above the praise and malice of all.

CHAPTER TWENTY-ONE

His Life and Conduct

THE LIFE and conduct of a perfect Master single him out as a unique personality apart from the rest of mankind.

1. He is always a bestower of gifts and never a recipient. He never wishes for the slightest service from his following. He earns his own living and is never a burden upon anyone. All his personal savings, if any, he spends on the relief of the needy.

> *Touch ye not the feet of one who makes his living out of the offerings of the people;*
> *O Nanak! he who earns his own bread and helps the needy knows the path.*

2. He does not charge any fees for imparting spiritual instructions. On the contrary, he bestows spirituality as a free gift like any other gift of God, such as light, air, water and so forth.

3. He is a living embodiment of humility. With all his powers and greatness co-equal with God, he never claims credit for anything, but attributes everything to God or to his own Master. Like a fruit-laden branch of a tree, he bows to the lowest, and moves about in simple dignity peculiar to him alone.

He who regards himself as the lowest is in fact the highest.

4. He is at peace with all and is angry with none. He smilingly forgives all who talk ill of him, and does not pick flaws in others. His love embraces all humanity. Christ-like, he proclaims and practices the cardinal truth, *Love thine enemies.*

5. Purity, Godliness and Spirituality flow from him like shining springs of cool and refreshing waters, bringing life to the parched and arid hearts of the aspirants who joyfully move along the Spiritual Path under his able guidance.

6. He does not wear any conspicuous form of dress. He adopts just an easy middle path. His Grand Trunk Road bypasses austerities on the one hand, and forms and formalities on the other. His teaching consists of enunciating natural truths which sink into the soul, and everyone irrespective of sex and age can practice the spiritual discipline enjoined by him.

7. He never believes in nor performs miracles for attracting people and gaining their credence, as a juggler would do. He keeps his treasures well concealed in the deepest recesses within him. He may, if necessity demands, make use of his powers on some special occasion. The disciples, of course, everyday feel the hidden hand of the Master working for their welfare and advancement.

CHAPTER TWENTY-TWO

The Physical Form of the Master

WE READ of peculiarities in the physical form of a perfect Master. Physically, too, he suffers from no deformity and has no weaknesses in him. His gait is full of grace and dignity. His eyes shine like those of a lion. He has a broad forehead, a mark of a lotus on his feet, and generally a black mole on his brilliantly luminous face.

Hafiz, a great Sufi poet of Shiraz, tells us:

> *If that beauty of Shiraz (the Master) were to take charge of my wandering mind, I would throw away both the worlds (earth and heaven) at the altar of the wonderful mole on His Face.*

CHAPTER TWENTY-THREE

The Influence of the Master

IN HIS PRESENCE, the mind grows docile and feels anchored.

> *How can we get the company of such a One by looking at whom the ever-restless mind gets lost, and Life Impulses swarm upon the soul? The Beloved Master makes a True Friend, and bestows God Intoxication.*

He sheds around him rays of purity, saturated with dignified humility, which exert a powerful influence upon the jivas. His words are charged with Spirituality and drag the soul into the beyond and administer a kind of living intoxicating exhilaration.

> *If he were to disclose his secrets, my very soul would swiftly soar Godward.*
>
> MAULANA RUMI

2. A steady gaze at his forehead and eyes reveals a peculiar Light which gives a pull to the soul and momentarily gathers up the all-pervading sensory currents, and one feels his being in higher Consciousness.

3. He is a Prince of Peace, and is above the pairs of opposites. His association releases in us currents of bliss and benediction. He dispels all thoughts of antagonism

and rivalry, and gives instead, equipoise to the soul, leading gradually to the Godhead.

In whose company one feels blessed, is the Master of Truth. He purifies the mind and grants salvation to the soul.

4. He is completely filled with the power of *ojas* (the fruit of chastity), and his forehead shines with Godly Light. One is irresistibly drawn by the magnetism of his charged words. From his eyes a peculiar Light shines forth, which like an osprey paralyzes the mind. He works like a leaven and quickens life in the desert of the mind.

5. With his lynx eyes, his gaze can penetrate deep into the feelings and emotions of a person; and he adjusts his instructions according to times and individual needs. The physical raiment of a jiva or soul is for him just like a transparent glass jar; though he can easily detect what is therein, he never exposes it to public view, and keeps his experience of each to himself. Whoever goes to him, whether a beetle or a wasp, gets sweet fragrance as from a flower. In the House of the Master, everything is in abundance, and each gets what he wishes for. Every person who contacts a Master Soul receives spiritual impressions which, in course of time, are bound to fructify. From the very moment an individual meets a Master, better times are assured to him.

6. A *Sant Satguru* is verily the Son of God. He has genuine love alike for persons of all religions, nationali-

ties and countries. He sees the Light of God in all. His appeal is therefore universal to all mankind.

> *All are born of the same Light, and as such there is no difference between man and man.*
> *O Nanak! people of all denominations flock into the fold of the Satguru.*
> *Satguru is all-merciful and all-knowing. He treats all alike, and does the work of all who have faith in him.*

He neither destroys the old church nor sets up another church of his own. He is a Master of Truth and does not care to what sect or creed a person may belong. All that matters is spiritual aspiration, for that alone befits a jiva for the Master's Path.

> *When one revels in Shabd or Word, he forgets all about himself.*
> *For the intelligent there is but One Path, no matter be he a Pundit or a Sheikh.*
>
> **KABIR**

He fearlessly talks of the Spiritual Path that lies within each one of us, in spite of our religious differences. One who is able to establish contact with such a Master is in fact a veritable pilgrim on the Path, and gets the greatest benefit from him.

Maulana Rumi, therefore, says:

> *Should ye be anxious for a pilgrimage, ye must take for a guide and companion any experienced pilgrim, no matter whether he be a*

> *Hindu, a Turk, or an Arab. Care not how he may look but see only that he is competent and knows the Path.*

We have, after all, not to establish any worldly relationship with the Master. All that we need from him is spiritual instruction and guidance, and if he can give us that, it should be considered enough.

7. Master Saints are the manifestation of Godhead. As heavenly truths dawn on them silently and subtly, so do their instructions work quietly, and sink into the very depths of the jivas without any word of mouth.

> *A Sheikh (Master), like God, is embedded in the formless Beyond, and he imparts his teachings without uttering a single syllable.*

The instructions of the Master are in a language that is speechless and can neither be imparted by word of mouth nor by word recorded.

> *Why do ye not understand my speech? Even because ye cannot hear my Word.*
>
> JOHN 8:43

Tongue of thought is his only instrument. It is a matter of inner experience for the spirit.

Maulana Rumi says:

> *Soul is of the same essence as that of God; it is God epitomized, and can express itself without any outer aid (like organs of speech).*

In the teaching of the Masters, physical senses are not of much avail. Everything is done automatically, despite the senses.

> *One sees without eyes, hears without ears, walks without feet, acts without hands, and talks without tongue; for this is just like Death-in-Life.*
> *O Nanak! it is then alone that one can know the Cosmic Will and meet the Beloved.*

Maulana Rumi also says the same thing:

> *I fly into those Regions without wings, travel there without feet; enjoy manna and elixir without lips and palate; and see the glories thereof by closing my eyes.*

8. The aspirants seldom have to question the Master to resolve their doubts, for the latter of his own accord explains things that are uppermost in the minds of the audience.

9. Time and again the teachings of the Master center around one theme: *Naam* or *Surat Shabd Yoga*. In clear terms they tell us that one cannot find God nor reach Him by engaging in outer pursuits, for He is the Lord of our very soul and must therefore be sought within, by the process of inversion.

Saint Matthew in his Gospel tells us:

> *Verily, I say unto you, Except ye be converted,*

and become as little children, ye shall not
enter into the kingdom of heaven.

MATTHEW 18:3

Again, in the Gospel of St. Luke, we have:

Verily I say unto you, Whosoever shall not receive the Kingdom of God as a little child shall in no wise enter therein.

LUKE 18:17

Great indeed is man, for his body is verily the Temple of God and the crest jewel of knowledge shines forth within.

Once again, St. Luke tells us:

The Kingdom of God cometh not by observation . . . the Kingdom of God is within you.

LUKE 17:20-21

A Muslim Divine speaks in similar strain:

The human heart is the Masjid (Mosque) and the body is the place of worship.

Again:

It does not befit a spirit (soul), the denizen of the God-made mosque (human body), to wander in search of the Beloved in man-made temples.

TULSI SAHIB

Magrabi Sahib also tells us:

Thy Beloved is within thee, and thou art ignorant of it. He is the very Soul of thy soul,

> and thou art wandering without in quest of Him.

Maulana Rumi in this context says:

> Within the folds of thy brain there are wonderful gardens and beauty spots. Should you like to enjoy them, hie to a Murshid (Master) for instruction.

> Those who search without for the inestimable Treasure are in stark ignorance. They wander in the bewildering mirage of the desert sands of the world, like a deer who runs about looking for musk in bushes.

The *Pind* (human body) is the exact replica of *Brahmand* (universe). The same spirit is working on both the microcosm and the macrocosm. We cannot see, feel, and be one with the Cosmic Spirit unless we establish harmony and come in touch with the spirit within us.

Until the embodied spirit becomes disembodied and rarified and rises above the sensual plane, it can hardly harmonize itself with Universal Spirit.

Nevertheless, our quest for God or Universal Spirit is all the time on the physical plane. We try to discover God under the bowels of the earth, on the snow-capped mountains, in the waters of the sacred rivers, and on desert sands; in man-made temples and mosques, in churches and synagogues; hence we fail to find Him.

If we know the inner Path in the body, we can hope to experience and feel the influence of the great power within. But this *inversion* or *conversion* is not possible without the aid of an adept in *Para Vidya* (Science of the Soul), for he alone holds the key to the Kingdom of God and his words act as an open sesame that fling open the secret door.

> *Just peep within as instructed by the Master, and thou shalt find within thyself a veritable Temple of God.*

10. The teachings of Master Souls are perfect, and their findings are as verifiable as in any other exact science.

This experience and realization is, however, quite different from book learning and intellectualism, nor is it a figment of an obsessed brain, as some think.

The Saints always talk with conviction and authority, for their utterances come from the depths of their souls. Their knowledge is neither derived from books nor based on hearsay testimony. They directly give us first-hand experiences of their own, in pure, unalloyed and unadulterated form. Again, they never ask for blind faith and acceptance on authority. On the contrary, each aspirant is asked to personally verify the result for himself.

Truth is that which must be experienced at once, and not after ages, no matter how slight that experience may be in the first instance. The Masters see things through to their very roots, and then talk.

> *Nanak sees God right before him.*

Sri Ramakrishna, being questioned by Naren (later known as Swami Vivekananda) about seeing God, replied, "Yes, my child! I have seen God as I see you."

In fact, all Master Souls have actual experience of the Godhead and they revel in His Light and Life and in a way become conscious co-workers with Him. Shamas-i-Tabrez says:

> *Better by far it is to see God with one's own eyes and to hear the Voice of God with one's own ears.*
>
> *His Glory is hidden behind the darkness at the back of the eyes and His Greatness may be apprehended within.*

In St. John we read:

> *When the dead shall hear the voice of the Son of God . . . they that hear shall live.*
>
> JOHN 5:25

Such great souls never depend on scriptures or sacred lore, which after all are recorded experiences of souls like them. They are truth personified, Word made flesh and living among us. All the Vedas and Shastras originate from the fountainhead within them. They are much more than the scriptures, which constitute but an infinitesimal speck of their personalities. The teachings of the Masters are very liberal, and help the embodied souls in the task of liberation and salvation.

> *I am the bread of life: he that cometh to me shall never hunger; and he that believeth on me shall never thirst.*
>
> JOHN 6:35

In *Melar-ki-war,* Guru Nanak tells us how to know a Master Soul:

> *He who can show us the Kingdom of God in this body is a Master Soul.*
> *He can attune our ears to the Voice of God.*
> *Even the grand divisions and minor divisions of the Universe are in perpetual ecstasy, for they live by the music emanating from the Seat of God.*
> *The Master exhorts the jivas to listen to this music in the Sukhman, the artery between the two eyebrows;*
> *Then be established in Sunnya (the Region of Silence), with the result that all oscillations of the mind would cease.*
> *When the chalice of the mind thus turns into the correct position, it will get filled with the Elixir of Life, making the mind steady and self-poised.*
> *The ceaseless music of eternity becomes a constant companion.*
> *All the aspirants attend to these five strains and in course of time become Gurumukh (the mouthpiece of the Guru), and attain the eternal abode of Truth.*
> *He who can with the aid of this music gain back the Garden of Eden (from which he has been exiled) is the beloved of God, and Nanak would wish to be his eternal slave.*

He never keeps his followers in delusion about the inefficacy of outer pursuits. His cardinal tenets center around one thing: contact with, and devotion to, Shabd alone. The manifestation of ceaseless music within is a gift of a Master Soul.

> *O Nanak! whoever contacts the perfect Master*
> *hears within himself the Divine Melody.*

Satguru is ever engrossed in Naam, and like a master pilot safely ferries bona fide aspirants across and leads them back to the Kingdom of God lost within them.

> *One dyed in the color of Naam is Satguru and,*
> *in Kal Yuga, he acts as Captain of a ship.*
> *He who confides and resides in him is carried*
> *across and finds Truth manifested in him.*

11. A Master Soul at times does uncommon things, that may appear baneful to ordinary individuals. This he does to keep the worldly-minded away from him, as one would do in the case of flies, so that they will not obstruct the way of true aspirants.

> *A darvesh (man of piety) needs no darwan*
> *(gateman);*
> *Yes, he does need one, to keep the dogs of the*
> *world away.*

An evil tongue or slanderer does work as a darwan for darveshes, so that the worldly-wise are kept out of the way.

In the biography of Bhai Bala it is on record that once Guru Nanak said:

> *In Kal Yuga many Saints or manifestations of God will come down, for the good of suffering humanity.*

Bhai Ajita questioned:

> *Master, will you tell us how we would know a perfect Saint; what would be his expression and how shall we recognize him?*

The Master replied:

> *Whenever a Saint appears, some leaders of society, religious bigots and caste-ridden individuals, talk ill of him. Rare indeed are those who go to him. The rank and file slander both the Master and his disciples. The people in general engage in outer pursuits, like reading scriptures, offering public prayers in churches, temples and mosques, and recitation of mantras, etc. They will not practice Surat Shabd Yoga by tuning with the primal Sound Current. When such conditions predominate, I will come time and again to revive the Path of the Masters and link people with Anhad Bani.*

12. With the advent of a Saint, the refreshing showers of Spirituality flood the dry and parched hearts encrusted with the dust of ages. Everyone who comes to him, whether a devotee or a sinner, derives benefit in

his own way and gets solace from him. Many a robber, murderer and highwayman has had a complete transformation in his company. Like a master washerman, he cleans our souls through and through of all impurities, bodily, mental and causal; until they shine forth in primal glory and become luminous and living selves.

We find in a Saint a living embodiment of selfless love and sacrifice. His appeal is universal and directed to the soul of man. The aspirants in thousands congregate around him and are benefited by his teachings.

13. A Saint is truly a Son of God and shares with Him all His Powers. His long and strong arm embraces the universe, and his helping hands extend to all parts of the world. Distance has no limitations for him. His saving grace miraculously works wonders in strange and unpredictable ways, and people escape unscathed from many a tense and hopeless situation, even from the jaws of death.

Master of earth and the heavens, he guides the spirits in their homeward journey through spiritual regions, and his Lustrous Form ever keeps company with the pilgrim soul as it transcends the body.

Maulana Rumi says:

The hand of a Master Soul is in no way shorter than that of God. It is in fact the Hand of God Himself.
Yes, it stretches across seven skies and inspires spirits with hope and confidence.

These are just a few of the innumerable signs that indicate a Saint.

Maulana Rumi says in this context:

> *An aulia (superman) has in him wonderful powers and possibilities, which a man of piety alone can see and experience.*

The glory and greatness of a Godman becomes more and more manifest to a spirit as it crosses over bodily and mental limitations and proceeds onward in his company. The Lustrous Form of the Master is ever with him now wherever he may be, guiding his footsteps both within and without, answering all his questions, the sole arbiter of his destiny—his very Saviour. It is at this stage that a person gets firmly established in him and cries out, *The Master is ever with me,* for now he realizes the truth of the Master's sayings:

> *Everyman, I will go with thee and be thy guide;*
> *In thy greatest need to be by thy side.*

The world is full of people who profess to be Masters and teachers of mankind. But all those who hanker after pelf and power, name and fame, cannot possibly play the role and perform this arduous duty, and one must try to avoid such false prophets, who are no less than ravening wolves in the garb of lambs.

It never pays to test and try a genuine Master. His very presence will of his own accord magnetize the mind. Maulana Rumi says:

> *None can subdue and still the oscillation of mind except through the overpowering influence of a Pir (Godman). Take thou a firm*

hold of such a person. If you are able to do this, it will be by his own grace and then his power will work in you.

He is an entity pure and desireless. Surrender your all at his feet; body, mind and attachments, and he will mold you to his fashion. How this can be done is the question.

Kabir Sahib tells us of the way:

Give thy body and mind to him who has no desire of his own;
With no thought of the self, be established in him;
After the mind, what then remains? Not even the body;
Nothing is left to be surrendered, says Kabir.
Having given the body and the mind, no burden remains to be carried;
He who takes pride in this sacrifice will yet have punishment;
For who can part with the seed-mind within?
O Kabir! How can that mind be subdued and surrendered?
Along with body and mind part thou with the seed-mind;
O Kabir! Only after hearing the Master, one becomes fearless;
Place the seed-mind at the altar of the Lotus Feet of the Master.
O Kabir! Now one sees nothing but the Luminous Form of the Master!

CHAPTER TWENTY-FOUR

Oneness of Guru, Guru Dev, Satguru and Malik
(THE VARIOUS FORMS OF TRUTH)

IN SCRIPTURES, we read that God is Formless. He sees without eyes and does His work without hands, moves about without feet and hears without ears.

He pervades everywhere, but cannot be seen. He is beyond all thought, comprehension and apprehension. Man with his limited intellect and finite understanding cannot reach Him. How then can we see God and love Him? Love and longing always exist betweeen creatures of the same class at one level. Birds of the air fly together in flocks; and there is love between animals of the same type, and they move about in herds. Man by nature is gregarious and cannot but live in society with his fellow beings.

Contemplation means concentration of human faculties at one center or focus. But if the center and the focus are not apparent and visible, how can there be any contemplation at all? To satisfy this fundamental need of mankind, Lord Rama and Lord Krishna (the manifestations of *Kal* or the Negative Power*) had to come in

---

* The same Power manifests in different ways to maintain life at various levels, just like electricity which produces fire at one place and ice at another.

the garb of man and so did Master Saints who manifest *Sat Purush* (the Positive Power)—Truth—the substratum of all that is visible and invisible, the entire universe with its grand divisions and subdivisions; right from Sach Khand or Muqam-i-Haq to Kal Desh, the physical world, which is subject to decay and death. A Muslim divine has beautifully described Him:

> *If He is Khud-aa (Self-Moving God), let Him come by Himself (to teach us).*

In fact, He has to come down to the level of man for then alone can man know of Him.

In the garb of a Master Saint, He works His Will by giving instructions to the souls that long for Him but cannot reach Him.

He tells them that He is not a physical body and He instructs all the embodied spirits how to transcend the limitations of the physical body, and by a gradual transmission of His power, He pulls them out of the physical raiment and becomes their friend and guide.

Thus the Formless has to assume a form, adopt a pole for the manifestation of His Godhead, for the suffering and helpless humanity; He tells us of our native worth and how to regain the lost Kingdom, the Garden of Eden, from which we have been exiled since the beginning of time.

God's power in fullness works at the pole of a Master Soul and he may therefore be truly described as polarized God come into the world with happy tidings to announce God and God's Kingdom, both of which he says are near at hand and can easily be gained by a little practice in the right direction.

He who has known Truth is Satguru. In fact, Satguru is *Sat* (Truth) personified. Word really becomes flesh and dwells among us, and by his instruction and guidance takes us along with him, until we, like him, become Word, a conscious principle working in harmony with the Divine Will on the Divine Plan.

> *Know ye for certain that Guru is not apart from God.*
> *Whatever his wishes, they are acceptable to God.*

CHAPTER TWENTY-FIVE

The Nature of Oneness

VERILY A SATGURU (Master of Truth) is one with *Sat* or Truth, as he is embedded in and revels in Truth. Truth is infinite and all-pervasive, while it manifests itself and works among people from a human pole —call it what you will: Master, Satguru, etc.

He is a beacon light that sheds the light of Truth on the tumultuous sea of life, to guide yearning humanity. He may be likened to a live switch that has behind it the entire energy of the powerhouse, but doles it out in such measure as may be needed by each individual according to his or her requirements.

Like a magnetized pole or a live switch, he possesses a raiment, but in fact is not the raiment, but the Power inside the raiment. Exactly so is the case of jivas or embodied spirits.

We too are in fact not what we possess and apparently seem to be—physical entities—but spirits or souls that enliven the physical bodies.

A spirit or soul is purely of the same essence and power that works in the Master, though clothed in countless raiments or sheaths and hedged in by numberless limitations.

But when it is able to transcend the various bodies and

become a spirit untrammeled and free, it can then witness the glory and greatness of the Master, for he is the horizon where the earth and heaven meet and the sun of God's Light rises and illumines all space.

A veritable sun lies hid in him.

We cannot have any adequate idea of God's beauty, grandeur and greatness by looking at the physical form of the Master. For an actual experience of Him, we have to rise to His level.

Unless we rise to the level of God, we cannot know of God.

As God is spirit, we too, by self-analysis, must be able to separate the spirit in us from the material sheaths or raiments enshrouding it, for spirit alone can see and experience spirit; not the physical senses nor even the intellect or mind.

The eyes of a Master are charmed casements that open within on Infinity and without on the finite. In them, one can get glimpses of Divine Light unparalleled in this world—a shadowless Light that never is found on sea or land.

Maulana Rumi tells us about him:

A Godman is ever in a state of intoxication without a drop of wine. He is ever satiated without a morsel of food.

His eyes are the eyes of God; his hands are the hands of God.

While living in the world, he is not of the world, nor is he a prisoner in the prison of the body, as we are. He is a free entity and at will crosses over into spiritual realms and is competent to grant this power and capacity to thousands of jivas, if he so wishes.

A living Master of Truth is one with Truth, and has in him Truth in fullness, whereby he carries on the work of salvation entrusted to him.

In spite of his form, he is formless. He is Word personified, a great fountainhead of love, bliss and peace. Man has to learn from man and, in accordance with this natural law, Word becomes flesh and dwells among us to impart spiritual instruction and guidance. Again, by transmitting his own life impulse he enables us to go homeward.

While doing this work among us, he every day at his sweet will escapes to his heavenly abode of Truth, so as to take rest in *Nij-anand* or imperishable bliss.

Master of Truth and Truth are one; for he is polarized Truth.

> *He is beyond everything, beyond Brahma, the*
> *primal principle;*
> *Nanak has met with such a Guru.*
> *The Master of Truth is eternally the same. He*
> *neither comes nor goes.*
> *He is the imperishable Life Principle that per-*
> *vades everywhere.*

With all our paeans in praise of the Master, we can never do justice to him; for he existed when nothing was and from him everything came into being at each cycle of creation.

> *Who can sing praises of the Master? He is the source of Truth.*
> *He is eternally unchangeable, the source of all life from age to age.*

In *Gurbani*, it is mentioned that after careful scrutiny within, one comes to an irresistible conclusion that Master is Truth and Truth is Master, with no distinction whatever between the two.

> *When churning the great sea within, one thing has come to the surface: Guru is Gobind and Gobind is Guru. O Nanak! There is no difference between the two.*

The Almighty in fact resides in the garb of a Saint and works His plan through him.

> *The Kartar (primal principle) resides in the Master and he becomes the means of salvation for many a soul.*

> *One knows nothing of love without a Master, for everyone is devoid of love. Hari resides in the Master, and blessed Master becomes the connecting link between a jiva and Hari.*

Kabir Sahib tells us that he is one with God:

> *Now I am one with Thee and feel satiated and blessed.*

> *Having reached the highest abode, I am one with Him; so much so that one cannot distinguish Kabir from Ram.*

Similarly, Shamas-i-Tabrez speaks in the same strain:

> *We have become so united, like body and soul, that hereafter no one can say I am different from Thee.*

Christ, too, says:

> *I and my Father are one.*
> JOHN 10:30
>
> *He that hath seen me hath seen the Father.*
> JOHN 14:9

God and Godman are indeed just like a sea and its tides. Momentarily as the tides rise and fall, they appear as something different, but they are of the same essence as the water of the parent sea.

Exactly the same is a drop of water. When separated from the sea it is a drop, but the moment it goes into the sea, it loses its apparent individuality and becomes part and parcel of the sea.

God is formless, while in Godman He assumes form for instruction and guidance of the people.

> *Nanak has after careful study of the Vedas and scriptures come to the conclusion that there is no difference between Parbrahm and* **Guru.**

God is the primal Sound Principle, which He gives to the thirsty through a Godman.

> *God resides in a Guru and releases the Sound Current among the aspirants.*
> *Established in Truth, Master revels in Truth.*
> *He is at once the Master of Truth and Truth itself.*
> *In every age, He comes down for the benefit of the devotees.*

In the Holy Bible, we read:

> *The Word was made flesh and dwelt among us ... full of grace and truth.*
>
> JOHN 1:14

In *Gurbani*, we have:

> *There is not the least distinction between Satguru and Swami (God-in-action and God).*
> *A contact with the former leads to devotion for the latter.*
>
> *A man of God is called Satguru or Sat Purush and he speaks of Hari alone; whoever listens to him attains salvation.*

Guru being one with the Almighty is the doer of everything and sustains the entire creation including the jivas.

> *Guru is the doer and does everything; he is the true Gurumukh.*
> *Guru is a conscious co-worker with God and is the sustainer of the entire creation.*

> *Guru is the bestower of peace and comfort and he is the Kartar (great motor power), O Nanak! We live and have our being in him alone.*

Gosain Tulsi Das, the celebrated author of the Hindi *Ramayana,* speaks of the Guru:

> *Salutation to the Lotus of the Guru, who is the ocean of mercy and God Himself in human form. His kindly words dispel in us the darkness born of blind attachments.*

In the Holy Bible, we read that Jesus once asked his disciples, "Whom do men say that I the Son of man am?" And Simon Peter answered and said: "Thou art the Christ, the Son of the living God." Jesus said to Peter:

> *Blessed art thou, Simon Bar-jona: for flesh and blood hath not revealed it unto thee, but my Father which is in heaven.*
> *And I say also unto thee, That thou art Peter, and upon this rock I will build my church; and the gates of hell shall not prevail against it.*
>
> MATTHEW 16:13, 16-18

On another occasion, he spoke more clearly to them:

> *Philip saith unto him, Lord, show us the Father and it sufficeth us.*
> *Jesus saith unto him, Have I been so long time with you, and yet hast thou not known me,*

> *Philip? He that hath seen me hath seen the Father; and how sayest thou then, Show us the Father?*
> *Believest thou not that I am in the Father, and the Father in me?*
>
> JOHN 14:8-10

Guru Arjan has in very explicit terms told us of his oneness with God:

> *My temples are in the highest heaven, and my Kingdom is limitless. My sway is eternal and countless is my wealth. My glory is known through the ages and my people live everywhere. I am worshiped by all and sundry and everyone is devoted to me. My Father is manifest within me and now the Father and the Son work together.*
>
> *O Nanak! The son has become a conscious co-worker with the Father and there is now no difference between the two.*

In the Hindu scriptures, we have:

> *Guru is Brahma, Guru is Vishnu, Guru is Shiva, and Guru is the veritable Par Brahm; and we offer our salutations to the Guru.*

In Mankukya Upanishad, it is stated:

> *As the various mountain streams after passing through different plains fall into an ocean and lose their names and separate existence, so do the knowers of Brahma merge in the*

> *Illustrious Self-Lustrous Being, losing their names and forms.*

Here a question arises as to how an all-pervading spirit can come to occupy a limited space in a human body. In Discourse 7 of the Bhagavad Gita, Lord Krishna thus sets at rest this question:

> *Not knowing my transcendent, imperishable, supreme character, the undiscerning think me who am unmanifest to have become manifest.*
>
> *Veiled by the delusive mystery created by my unique power, I am not manifest to all; this bewildered world does not recognize me, birthless and changeless.*
>
> SHALOKS 24-25

Again, in Discourse 9, Shalok 11, the Blessed Lord says:

> *Not knowing my transcendent nature as the Sovereign Lord of all beings, fools condemn me incarnated as man.*

Muslim divines also seem to corroborate this, according to Maulana Rumi:

> *The arm of a Pir (Master) is in no way shorter than that of God, and the veritable Power of God works through the former. His long arm stretches as far as the seventh heaven; his hand is in the hand of God and no one besides him shows His greatness. In fact, an*

effulgent sun lies hid in him and the greatest good lies in knowing him, as he is.

Again, the Maulana says:

The Light of Truth shines in the heart of a Wali (Godman). If you are a momin (Guruman) you may see this as it is.

The Prophet once declared that God Himself told him that He far transcended the highest heights, the lowest depths, the earth, the sky and all the heavens; but strange as it might seem, He could comfortably rest in the heart of His devotees, and he who wished to meet Him could find Him there.

Though he (the Murshid) lives on the earth, yet his soul spreads out in the limitless beyond, which all reasoning and philosophy of the religious cannot reach.

Shamas-i-Tabrez tells us in this wise:

The King of Kings is enthroned in us, behind a dense curtain. In the vile garb of flesh, He comes to grant us access to Himself.

Bulleh Shah says:

Maula (God) becomes man so as to pull men up (from their deep slumber).

We have in Gurbani many references to this effect.

God Himself assumed the name of Ram Das.*

* The fourth Guru of the Sikhs.

> *Greatly intelligent is our God. He Himself assumes and takes for Himself the title of a Saint.*
>
> *O Pipa! Pranva (the Sound Current) is the only Reality, and becomes embodied as a Satguru for our instruction and guidance.*
>
> *Satguru is Niranjan (pure, immaculate); do not consider him as a human being.*
> *A devotee of the Lord himself becomes the Lord, but man knows not this mystery.*

Bhai Gurdas likewise says:

> *Ek Onkar (the one God unmanifest) becomes Akar (the manifest) and assumes the appellation of a Guru.*

He who can tell you of the Reality (impersonal) and put you in contact with Reality (Truth eternal and unchangeable permanence), is no other than personal Reality (Truth personified). He truly is the primal Sound Current emanating from the Most High.

In order to teach mankind, this Sound Current becomes materialized in the form of Saints. How else can men have spiritual instruction unless the Spirit of God, which the Sound Current is, takes a human form and lives among them, talks to them face to face of mysteries both human and divine? This is why Kabir says:

> *Brahma cannot speak as Brahma alone. He too needs a human agency for His self-expression (among human beings). We, as human entities*

encased in flesh and bones, cannot have an idea of that attributeless Formless One, unless He assumes a likeness to our own, on this material plane, and becomes for us a living God capable of being seen, heard and understood. He is at once both God and man, and may be called Godman. He works as a means to an end, a link between man and God. He is Word personified so that He may impart instructions about God and guidance toward God.

Peter the Great, Czar of Russia, was anxious to learn shipbuilding and the art of navigation, so he went to Holland disguised in the garb of an ordinary laborer. In the Dutch dockyards there were many other Russian laborers, working for their living, and Peter worked with them, talked to them of Russia their native land, and often asked them to return with him.

These poor people were exiles from their country and would heave sighs because they could not go back however much they wished. Peter told them that the mighty Czar himself was known to him, and he might be able to secure them a pardon. But very few could imagine that a person in tattered clothes like their own could have anything to do with the Czar.

When Peter started on the journey homeward, after completing his training, just a few who believed his words accompanied him. When he entered Russia, he was received royally from place to place. When the outlawed laborers saw the honor given Peter, they felt encouraged and confident that he would be able to have the Czar reverse the decree of outlawry against them. When at last they saw Peter enter his capital and ascend the throne, they were astounded at the change in their co-laborer.

The Master, like Peter the Czar, is the King of Kings. He comes into the dockyard or prison-house of this world just as an ordinary laborer or prisoner like us. He also earns his living as we do, talks to us of our native land, infuses in us a longing and desire to return home, and offers to be our companion and guide on the way. A few who put faith in his words begin to act on his advice, and they are taken out of this vast prison back to the throne of God, where they find the Master in his Radiant Form, more lustrous than thousands of suns and moons put together.

Guru Arjan tells us that He who sent us into exile is now calling us back to His Kingdom as His true inheritors and legatees.

Again, when Queen Indra Mati completed her course of spiritual discipline and reached Sach Khand, she found her Master, Kabir, in the seat of Sat Purush (the True God). Seeing this, she said, "Master! Why did you not tell me before that you were Sat Purush yourself? I would have believed you." Kabir, smiling, replied, "I could not have convinced you then."

All Saints who reach Sat Lok or Anami Desh become one with God and as such rank equal to each other; and none can be said to be greater than the other.

> *He who tries to distinguish a Saint from a Saint starts headlong for hell.*

Generally, thousands of people congregate around a Satguru and listen to his discourses, but each one sees him according to his own mental and spiritual make-up. Some consider him as a person of piety; some take him for a philosopher, and some as just a man of learning. Others regard him as an ideally moral man, and still others as a selfless worker. Rare indeed are the jivas who find God in him.

Thus each one finds in him a reflection of what he himself actually is or wishes to become, and so gets from him that quality, for he distributes to each what he merits.

As a man in physical raiment his foremost duty, of course, is man-making; and as God personified it is revealing or manifesting God. So it all depends on one's own preparedness through the ages. Blessed indeed is the man who is ready for immediate transformation into God, for to such an individual he at once reveals his Godhood; as Krishna revealed his oneness with Kal to Arjuna, when through ignorance he hesitated to perform his duty as a Kshatriya prince.

A blind man cannot see one with eyes nor can he take hold of him, unless the man with sight compassionately takes him by the hand and leads him aright.

Similarly, no one can see in a Master the Master of Truth or Truth itself lodged in him unless he reveals his real self to him. Even those who constantly live with him, including his close relatives, can seldom recognize in him the hidden Godhead.

Without the gift of special merit one can never know

of the really intrinsic nature of a Saint (his Godhood). He who can see and recognize God in him has indeed found God, for He not only resides in him but manifestly works through him.

He is the pole from where the power of God shines forth and works out the Divine Will.

Bhai Nandlal says:

> *God is ever present before thee; see thou His blessed form.*

Guru Nanak similarly says:

> *The God of Nanak is ever before him.*

In the same way, when Naren (later Swami Vivekananda) first met Sri Ramakrishna, he asked him, "Master, have you seen God?" And Ramakrishna replied, "Yes, my child! I have seen Him as I see you."

Thus it all depends on our inner vision. If one is gifted with this, or if Satguru so wishes, he may see the flashes of God's Light coming through the Master. The purpose of all spiritual discipline is the restoration of the lost vision to the inner eye, so that we may be able to see God, both as all-pervading in the Universe and as deeply concentrated behind the mighty breakwater of the Master.

This revelation then depends upon the sweet will of God and no one can claim it as a right. It is just a pure and simple gift from Him to one who has prepared himself through the ages.

CHAPTER TWENTY-SIX

The Blessings of God and the Master

THE PATH OF SPIRITUALITY is not a highway that one may tread easily. It is an arduous and an uphill task, tortuous and difficult.

In Katha Upanishad, we find:

Awake, arise and get illumination by sitting at the feet of Masters. The wise say this way is sharp as a razor and as difficult to walk on.

Farid, a Muslim divine of great repute, says:

O Farid! Get up and tread the world over in search of some Godly man, for then alone can you be truly blessed.

In the Holy Koran this path is termed *Pul-i-Sirat,* and is described as "sharp as a razor's edge" and "narrow as a hair."

Bhai Gurdas also speaks of *Gur Sikhi* (Master's Path) in the same words, "narrower than a hair and sharper than a razor's edge."

Because strait (narrow) is the gate, and narrow is the way, which leadeth unto life, and few there be that find it.

MATTHEW 7:14

In the Vedas, too, there are texts prescribing countless rules and regulations for the performance of yogic *asans* and *sadhans* so difficult that the thought of them makes one's hair stand on end.

With such hardships ahead, how can a puny child of clay, powerless as he is, constantly ridden by mind and matter, entangled in the meshes of blind infatuation and beset with desires, anger, greed, attachment and egoism, escape unscathed by himself and become a successful pilgrim on the Path?

In such a weird setting, all baffling and bewildering, with no way out, God takes mercy on His creatures. He Himself comes down in vile man's attire, to suffer woe so that His children may be blessed. But again the same trouble confronts us.

To understand the teachings of the Master and strictly follow them from day to day, to confide in him and to completely surrender one's self, body and soul, to his will, is not an easy thing to do. Unless God and Satguru both take pity on a jiva, he cannot possibly see through to Reality and escape from bondage.

Himself the Master of the Universe, He may draw in a jiva, and effect a union.

We with our limited understanding cannot even listen comprehendingly to the Master's words.

But in the fullness of time when it so pleases God, He brings about a meeting between a jiva and a Sant Satguru, who establishes his contact with Naam—the power of God or God in action—the Primal Sound Current, wherewith a jiva is gradually led on and on until he reaches the source and the fountainhead of Shabd or the Sound Current.

> *Those who serve not Truth wither away like a broken reed,*
> *O Nanak! Whom the Master blesses gets linked with Naam.*
> *With a special merit alone one meets a Satguru; and he brings about a union between Surat and Shabd.*
> *Meeting with a Master is a pure gift of God, and so is the union with Hari Nam* (God).

The Master is in the likeness of God, though in physical raiments. He, too, is endowed with the same attributes as God Himself. He, too, comes to save the sinners and administer His Saving Grace among the rest. He washes the jivas clean of their sins and gives the gift of Naam, which acts as a sovereign remedy against all ills, physical, accidental and spiritual.

> *My Master takes away all sins and I depend on him. Forgive all my trespasses, O Master! Nanak prays for this alone.*
> *Great are the blessings of a perfect Master. With the worship of Hari comes eternal bliss.*
> *The union with the Lord is the gift of a perfect Master. Eternally forgiven, I now soar limitless and free.*

The seventeenth century English poet Dryden, speaking of Christ, tells us:

> *See God descending in thy human frame; the offended, suffering in the offender's name.*
> *All thy misdeeds to Him imputed see; and all His righteousness devolved on thee.*

The grace of the Master is as limitless as his greatness, so much so that he forgives even those who talk ill of him and accepts them as his very own.

> *One who talks ill of the Master may yet turn around,*
> *To find his saving grace leading him to his fold.*

Countless are the persons whose sins are forgiven and are safely ferried across the sea of life.

> *With Shabd he burns to ashes the Karmic impressions of many a soul;*
> *Like a Captain, he pilots the ship through many a shoal.*

The Master truly is God. He is a sea of heaving compassion. All kinds of gifts eternally flow from him like perennial springs of cool and refreshing water.

> *Narain (Creator) in Guru is compassion incarnate and a true friend;*
> *In his pleasure is everything, and Nanak is a sacrifice unto him.*

The greatest gift of God and Guru is just one thing—

Naam. They always bestow upon their devotees the blessings of Naam, and thus bring about their salvation.

> *Devotees of God ever revel in Naam; with saving grace they ever march on.*
> *The very sight of Him is a rare blessing; the truly blessed can have it; with the mercy of the Merciful, Satguru confers the gift of Naam.*

In this world and hereafter, there is no gift greater than that of Naam.

> *Priceless is the treasure of Naam; a True One may grant it at his will.*

One can secure the gift of Naam and thereby find an approach to God through Satsang and Satguru.

> *Whomever the Master may bless, he may have the Love of the Lord.*
> *The compassion of God comes into commotion when one is truly blessed by a Sadh, O Nanak.*

The saving grace comes through *contact* with Naam, and *continuous cherishing* of His love and saving grace in turn helps the other way. Both grace and Naam work in reciprocity and help in developing each other.

> *O Nanak! Naam comes from grace alone.*
> *There is no friend other than Ram Naam.*
> *Getting above the pairs of opposites, stick to Naam and He shall bless.*

> *The moment I forget Truth, that moment is wasted.*
> *Remember Him with every breath, and His grace shall be with us.*

His grace descends by acceptance of His *bhana* (will) and recognition of His *hukam* (commandment).

> *He who knows His hukam has no occasion to regret;*
> *O Nanak! engrave the gift of His Naam on thy soul.*

The seed of Naam, once sown by a Saint, cannot but fructify—no power can stop it; and the jiva must sooner or later reach the goal, viz., self-realization and God-realization.

> *Truth one gets through grace alone; none has the power to stop Its growth.*
> *Naam is watered by death-in-life, and Gurumukhs do it; God grants them this treasure and none can snatch It.*

Even *Kal* (Time) and *Maya* (Delusion) can have no effect on the seed of Naam, for It is conceived in a region much higher than their domains.

Besides, the sower of the seed—the Satguru—is *Sat Purush* Himself (His manifested form); and so Ishwar (*Niranjan*, Lord of the Subtle Region) and Parmeshwar (*Om*, Lord of the Causal Region) cannot interfere in his work.

> *The gift of the Guru is eternal; It has the saving grace for the recipient.*
> *The Shabd of the Master reigns supreme, O Nanak! The Master is no one but God.*

The blessings of the Supreme Lord are limitless and do not at any time suffer from scarcity, but one partakes of them only by extraordinary merit. A particle of grace is enough to save a jiva from the ceaseless cycle of transmigration.

> *Once He showers His blessings, there is an end to endless births;*
> *As comings and goings cease, one at home finds eternal rest.*

It is only the Gurumukhs who get this grace and not the manmukhs.

> *O Nanak! He does all by Himself, and Gurumukhs enjoy His favor.*
> *The bitter words of the Master taste sweet;*
> *His sweet words are a boon all his own;*
> *His words, whatever they are, bear fruit in abundance,*
> *But the idle words of others go in vain.*

One works out Naam through His grace alone.

> *Thy grace alone helps in developing the power of Naam;*
> *Without any shortcomings, one ever engages in Naam.*

Man by himself is just a helpless creature and can do nothing. He must not therefore feel vainglorious for what he seemingly does.

God alone is the Doer of all acts; He knows the innermost secrets of all hearts.

The panacea for all ills and the only way to win God's grace is perfect surrender in all humility at the feet of the Master Soul.

CHAPTER TWENTY-SEVEN

The Solicitude of the Master

THE RELATIONSHIP of the Master and the disciple is unique in character and we find no parallel to it on earth. Still, Saints have tried to make us understand something of it. While all worldly connections and ties are more or less tainted by selfishness, the relation between the Master and the disciple is purely one of selfless love.

Just for the sake of analogy, we may consider the love of a mother for her child. An infant at birth is just a mere helpless mass of tender flesh and bones. He cannot express himself and his needs, nor can he look after himself, but the mother takes tender care of the tiny piece of humanity. She attends to his every need and looks after his comforts. In his happiness lies her happiness and in his sorrow she feels distressed. Day and night she tirelessly works for the child's welfare and does not consider any sacrifice too great. She denies herself everything so that her child may have all that she can afford to give and is ready even to lay down her life for his sake.

As the infant grows, he begins to imbibe his mother's love. The kindly rays of love pass from eyes to eyes. In mute language he begins his first lessons in love. Gradually, the toddler is taught to speak, at first in broken syllables, and the mother's delight knows no bounds at every success in her endeavors, until he grows big enough to look after himself.

In exactly the same way, when a person is accepted by the Master he takes a second birth, as it were, into the Master's house. He comes into the Master's fold full of worldly attachments and dyed deep in the darkest shades of mind and matter. He is so identified with his body and bodily relations that he can never think that he is something apart from them.

With all his worldly wisdom, whatever riches, name and fame he may have, he is blank in matters spiritual. Having lived all his life on a sensual plane, he is conscious of nothing but sense pleasures which are the end and all for him.

With his birth in the Master's house, the Master takes upon himself an immense load of responsibility. By individual instructions and attention, he gradually weans the jiva from sense pleasures. He tells the disciple that he is neither body nor mind nor intellect, but something more glorious—soul or spirit—and has been endowed by Nature with various faculties to serve a high purpose in life. By spiritual discipline, the Master enables him to free his mind of mental oscillations. Now he develops a state of equipoise, and with it he begins to evaluate life from a different angle. His entire outlook is changed and a consciousness of spirit dawns in him.

He is no longer a slave of his senses engaged in sensual pursuits, but finds an inner satisfaction, peace and serenity which keeps him engrossed all the time at the seat of the very Self. All this is the work of the Master, and much more besides. To wash clean a jiva from the impurities of the world is no mean task, but it is absolutely necessary for a spiritual life.

He has to be pulled up from his senses, mind and intellect, and this no one but a Master can achieve.

To stop the course of the mighty rush of sensory currents flowing headlong into the world, and to hold them at one center, is a gigantic task in itself. The next job of the Master is even more important than this.

After the preliminary cleansing process, he pulls scales from the inner eye and gives it vision and Light; and he breaks the seal on the inner ear, making the jiva hear the inner music of the soul. By his individual attention and care he makes an adept out of trash and scrap—capable of understanding and enjoying the unspoken language and unwritten law of God, and of doing actions without the aid of outer organs and faculties.

The Master takes care of the disciple with his own life impulse.

> *Blessed indeed is the Master, who by his instructions purifies us through and through.*
> *Satguru cuts asunder all the shackles of the disciples.*

As Wordsworth sang of his sister, so a disciple sings of his Master:

> *She gave me eyes; she gave me ears;*
> *and humble cares and delicate fears;*
> *A heart the fountain of sweet tears,*
> *and love and thought and joy.*

The Master always saves his disciples, no matter how dangerous a situation they may be in. His protecting arms serve as a shield and buckler, and the disciple leads a charmed life, as it were. The Master does all this simply because he has taken charge of a jiva; there is no obligation on the disciple's part, nor does he necessarily know about it.

Again, the Master takes upon himself the burden of his disciples' sins and iniquities.

> *All thy misdeeds to Him imputed be*
> *And all His righteousness devolved on thee.*
>
> DRYDEN

He takes in his own hands the entire process of winding up the karmic impressions of the jiva. Having freed him from the sensual plane by reversing his sensory current so that it flows upward, the Master renders him incapable of sowing any more karmic seeds for future harvesting; and whatever trespasses he may still commit through weakness of the flesh, the Master himself gently and firmly deals with here on earth, leaving no debit balance to be carried forward. In this way, the account of *Kriyaman* karma (present deeds) is settled and squared.

Next come the *Pralabdha* karmas, which determine what we call fate or destiny, and because of which we come into the world. The Master does not touch them and happily the disciple weaves his way through their spell.

> *Through the compassion of the Lord all trials*
> *and tribulations fly;*

Satguru himself saves a jiva from all harm.

Last but not least, the Master feeds the jiva with the Bread of Life and quenches his thirst with the Water of Life (Naam) until he grows into spiritual adolescence and is capable of a certain amount of self-reliance. The touch of the spark of Naam (God-in-Action or the controlling power of God) burns out the storehouse of unfructified karma of ages upon ages (*Sanchit* or storehouse), thus rendering them incapable of germinating in the future.

Satguru keeps his sikh (disciple) on manna and elixir;
So very kind is the Master to his disciple.

I am the bread of life; he that cometh to me shall never hunger; and he that believeth on me shall never thirst.

JOHN 6:35

The protective care of the Master is much more than that of a mother for her child. He ever keeps his loving eyes on his disciple and guards him from all that is harmful, for his love knows no bounds.

As a mother tends her child and ever looks after him;
Gives him food and nourishment for growth all around;
So does the Master look after his beloved with Godly love.

> *As mother loves the child, and fish the water,
> so does Master love his own man.*

In this respect, distance is of no consequence and it does not count with the Master. His long and strong arm can reach everywhere, and his penetrating gaze can pierce through all space.

> *His hand is the hand of God, and the power of
> God works through him.*
>
> MAULANA RUMI

Wherever a disciple may be, however extreme his outer circumstances, the Master is always with him and guides him at every step, for that is his eternal promise:

> *Everyman, I will go with thee and be thy
> guide;
> In thy most need to go by thy side.*

A skylark is a pilgrim of the skies, and yet she hatches her eggs by giving them her whole attention. Similarly, the Master always keeps his disciple within his gaze, nurtures him with the Water of Life—the seed of Naam sown in the seeker's soul—until the spirit is able to break through the triple-shelled egg (physical, astral and causal sheaths) and shines forth in her own self-radiance.

> *O Nanak! Master takes care of the disciple
> with his very life impulse;
> He keeps him safe in his own hands and looks
> after him all the time.*

Love alone is the cementing force that binds the Master

and the disciple. Through unbounded compassion he delivers God's message to suffering humanity and prays that they may be saved from the imperceptible fire in which all are being consumed.

Maulana Rumi says:

> *He calls the people toward the Kingdom of God;*
> *He prays to God for their forgiveness and salvation.*

Satguru is the real friend of the disciple. He saves him from tense and hopeless situations. He comes to his aid when he has despaired of all hope and relief, and is surrounded by seemingly powerful forces arrayed against him. From time to time the disciple feels the overpowering influence of the Master working for his good. At times he works in ways that are difficult for the disciple to understand. Just as a mother waits in the early morning hours for her sleeping child to awaken, in the same way, even more anxiously, the Master looks forward wistfully to the time when his disciple, steeped in deep ignorance born of matter and mind, will raise his head, look toward him and gladden his heart.

The loving care of the Master becomes more manifest at the time of the disciple's final leave-taking from the world. While all his relatives and friends helplessly wait beside the sickbed, and the doctors declare the case hopeless, the Luminous Form of the Master appears to take charge of the departing spirit and guide it to the new world, to the judgment seat of God.

After that, he takes it to whatever region he thinks best, for further discipline and advancement on the path.

> *Serve the real Satguru and secure tightly the riches of Truth;*
> *At the last moment he shall come to thy rescue.*
> *He alone is a friend who accompanies me on my last journey, and stands by me before the judgment seat of God.*
> *My Master is all in all and the source of all comforts.*
> *He links me with the transcendent Brahma and comes to my aid at the last.*

Maulana Rumi says:

> *O ignorant fool! Quickly take hold of a guide; for then wilt thou be saved from the horrors of the beyond.*

All our worldly ties and connections are of an ephemeral character. Some leave us in poverty, some in adversity, some in illness. A few may stay beside us all through life, but they too fall away at the time of death. But Satguru is the real friend, who always overshadows the disciple and keeps his protecting arms around him wherever he may be. He stands by him at the time of his death and even goes along with his spirit as a guide to the other worlds.

> *O Nanak! Snap asunder all ties of the world, and find some friendly Saint;*
> *World attachments shall leave thee even in life,*

> *while the Other shall stand steadfast unto death and beyond.*

A soul awakened to Reality by a Satguru cannot be a prey to the messengers of death but must go with the Radiant Form of the Master, which comes to receive it when it casts off its physical raiment.

Kabir Sahib tells us that gold does not rust, nor steel eaten by worms; so a disciple of the Master, no matter how good or bad, never goes to hell.

> *Gold attracts not rust nor steel the worms;*
> *The disciple of the Master will never go to hell.*

The Master is the Master indeed, both in this world and the next, and helps a jiva in both the worlds. There is no greater friend.

> *I have taken hold of my Hari; He is my sustainer and is ever with me.*
> *He is a guardian angel in both the worlds; for almighty and ever merciful is the Satguru.*
> *I have with me Satguru, who helps me in all my needs; blessed is the Satguru, who reveals God to me.*
> *There is no friend greater than Satguru; he is the Protector, here and everywhere.*

If and when a jiva comes across a Satguru, he may thank his God, for the Guru underwrites life eternal for him. Full of compassion as he is, he unhesitatingly helps him through difficult situations, and without the least thought of obligation.

Maulana Rumi says of him:

Kind hearted and selfless is the friend;
He helps in dire difficulties and hard times.

The Guru is pledged to help the helpless. Through sheer compassion he extends his saving grace to all humanity. His company is the most beneficial; with Guru by his side, one may successfully defy millions of enemies.

When Guru is thy shield and buckler, millions
of hands cannot strike thee down.

Truly blessed are the jivas who have had access to the charmed precincts of the Satguru, for they have nothing to worry about here or hereafter.

The world bows to him in adoration; regions
divine anxiously await his advent;
For perfect is he who is in touch with the
Perfect.

How very very fortunate are the disciples who are under the shadow of his holy wings; in their lifetime and beyond they march with leaps and bounds on the grand trunk road of spirituality.

CHAPTER TWENTY-EIGHT

Master and the Controlling Power

SATGURU is the fountainhead of grace. Strange are the ways in which he works his grace. With just a single kindly look he may bless a jiva forever. He showers Naam in abundance. Should he in his pleasure place his blessed hand on the head of a jiva, the latter wishes for no other blessing.

In the twinkling of an eye, the jiva penetrates through the dark veil of ignorance and experiences the power of his grace—the Divine Light and the Divine Music—both of which become manifest to him. The contact with these at once wipes off the otherwise indelible karmic impressions of many ages, and the jiva attains life eternal, full of grace and peace.

> *My Friend has blessed me with peace, for he has manifested the Sound Current within;*
> *My Friend has shown God to me by a touch of his hand.*
>
> *With the touch of the Guru's hand, God has blessed me with the pearl of Naam;*
> *The sins of ages have vanished—such is the power of Naam.*

Rare indeed are the jivas who are fortunate enough to be blessed like this by the Master's hand.

> *Worship one who has the treasure of God with him;*
> *Blessed is the jiva who has the Master's hand on him.*
>
> *Blessed indeed is the touch of the Master's hand,*
> *Which one in millions is fortunate enough to get.*

In all the wide world the touch of the Master's hand helps the jiva in his trials and tribulations, and he becomes free from care. The entire world bows and bends at his feet in silent adoration. He can freely go to the various divisions of the creation at his sweet will and pleasure, for the grace of the perfect Master makes him perfect as well.

> *With his hand over one's head, his power extends on all sides;*
> *His grace opens the way to the spiritual realms, ending all ills.*

CHAPTER TWENTY-NINE

Surrender to the Master

SURRENDER to the feet of the Master means to merge one's individual will in the will of the Master, and to completely place oneself at his mercy. It is the surest and easiest way to escape from all cares and anxieties. It comes only when a disciple has complete faith and confidence in the competency of the Master.

This type of self-surrender is like that of a completely helpless patient who, trusting in the skill of a competent surgeon, places his life in his hands and quietly submits himself to his knife and lancet.

Or it may be compared to the trust given by the hopelessly lost traveler in the wilderness to the forest ranger who finds him and leads him out.

In exactly the same way, the work of the Master does not consist in merely teaching the theory of Para Vidya (Science of the Beyond), but it includes the practical demonstration of results of spiritual experiments, and help and guidance through all the disciples' difficulties. A true friend does not only give theoretical lessons in how to escape from mind and matter; he helps in effecting the escape itself.

Suppose, for instance, that a person has to go abroad. He will begin by making inquiries as to the various means of transportation available, land, sea or air, as he may choose. After he makes his choice he enters the plane, ship or train, and relying on the skill of the operator, takes his seat comfortably without the least anxiety. Should the ship flounder, or the plane be caught in a storm, it is the duty of the captain or pilot to take every possible care to save the conveyance along with the passengers for whom he is responsible.

In exactly the same way, an aspirant for spirituality has, after careful investigation, to decide first about the spiritual worthiness of a Master, and then to submit himself wholly and solely to his authority and direction without any mental reservations whatever; for he alone knows the turns and twists of the spiritual path and is in a position to act as an unerring guide.

The term *surrender* therefore means that a disciple should have full confidence in the skill and competence of the Master, and scrupulously follow and act on his instructions whatever they may be, whether in conformity with his own reason or not—for his reason being limited may be faulty or fall far short of the depth or prove uncertain.

It is not for him to question the propriety of the Master's commandments. He must learn, like a soldier, to obey his command without knowing the why and wherefore of things; for the Master knows what is best and most suitable in each case.

One must therefore obey the Master literally, and straightway engage himself in the sadhan or spiritual practice and discipline as it may be laid down for him.

This is the only way to spiritual success; there is no other.

In this context, we have the testimony of Hafiz, a great Sufi poet of Persia, who declared:

> *Dye thy prayer carpet in wine should the Master so desire;*
> *For he is not ignorant of the turns of the highway ahead.*

When a disciple entrusts his all to the Master, he becomes carefree and the Master has of necessity to take over the entire responsibility; just as a mother does for her child who does not know what is good for him.

As the disciple develops in his sadhan, he fits himself to receive more grace from the Master. Under his kind and benign influence, the disciple begins to thrive from day to day, and all his wishes are fulfilled without the least trouble on his part.

> *Sages and seers cry from the housetops:*
> *Ye seekers after peace, hie to a Master Saint.*

In Discourse 17, Verse 66, of the Bhagavad Gita, the Blessed Lord Krishna as a world teacher announces:

> *Abandon all duties and come to me, the only refuge; I will deliver thee from all sins: grieve not.*

In the Holy Koran, we have likewise:

> *Whosoever surrenders his purpose to Allah while doing good, his reward is with his*

> *Lord, and no fear shall come upon him, neither shall he grieve.*
>
> 2.112; 10.6

And in the Bible:

> *And I will turn my hand upon thee and purely purge away thy dross, and take away all thy tin.*
>
> ISAIAH 1:25

> *Come unto me, all ye that labor and are heavy laden, and I will give you rest.*
>
> MATTHEW 11:28

Also:

> *Call upon me in the day of trouble; I will deliver thee.*

Self-surrender is not an easy task. To accomplish it, one has to recede back to the position of an innocent child. It means an entire involution, a complete metamorphosis, supplanting one's own individuality.

It is the path of self-abnegation, which not everyone can take.

On the other hand, the path of spiritual discipline is comparatively easy. Self-effort can be tried by anyone in order to achieve spiritual advancement.

It is, no doubt, a long and tortuous path, as compared with the way of self-surrender, but one can, with confidence in the Master, tread it firmly step by step. If, however, a person is fortunate enough to take to self-surrender, he can have all the blessings of the Master quickly; for he goes directly into his lap and has nothing to do by himself for himself.

He is then the Master's Elect, his beloved son, the son of God Himself. But very rarely even a really blessed soul may be able to acquire this attitude.

> *Should the Lord so ordain, then, O Nanak!*
> *a person may take the path of self-surrender.*
> *Blessed indeed is one who surrenders at the feet of the Satguru;*
> *Standing near Truth he revels in Truth and easily merges in Truth,*
> *O Nanak! It is by the Lord's grace that one may meet such a Gurumukh.*

In the scriptures one finds a large number of advantages from adopting this path:

> *All ills and sorrows vanish by surrender at the Master's feet.*
> *In the world of joys and sorrows, he alone escapes who gains the feet of the Satguru;*
> *A Gurumukh stands apart from the three gunas and is acceptable to the Lord.*
> *In self-surrender the mind becomes purified; but chanting of God's name alone does not help.*
> *For the world's good do those come who thirst for a sight of Him;*
> *He who surrenders makes a clean escape, with desires all fulfilled.*
> *All joys lie with Satguru; bow then at his feet;*

> *blissful is the very sight of him.*
> *With no regrets chant paeans unto him.*
> *I see the world being consumed in the fire of egoism. Escape thou by surrender to the Master, and then attend to True Shabd.*
> *I surrender to One who alone is the cause, both material and efficient. His grace has shown the native land in the light of the moon.*
> *With a Life Impulse from a perfect Master, Ram Naam rests in me;*
> *O Nanak! With a surrender to the Master's feet the Lord Himself becomes merciful.*
> *In Kali Yuga Naam lies hidden everywhere, and the Lord in fullness pervades;*
> *But the precious Naam becomes manifest in that surrender to the Master.*

With the blessings of the Guru one becomes fearless of death and is successfully ferried across the sea of life.

> *He happily conquers death and never goes to hell. O Nanak! He is saved by surrender, for Hari just takes him into His care.*

Having been accepted by the Acceptor, all his acts become pure.

> *O Nanak! Never will he go to hell; such is the gift of surrender.*
> *None but the Elect engage in the devotion of Naam. O Nanak! With surrender at the*

*Master's feet one never comes and goes.
The dispeller of ills and Lord of all is attained through surrender to a Sadh; and the tumultuous sea of life is ferried across quickly.*

When a jiva surrenders to the Satguru, the Lord takes him under His own protection and grants unto him the blessings of *Sehaj* (eternal happiness). All doubts and fears now disappear and he comes to his own real Self.

CHAPTER THIRTY

The Words of the Master

WHEN A PERSON comes to a Master, he must come with an open-minded outlook. Since he knows that all his actions hitherto, individual as well as social, have not so far secured him salvation, he should bid goodbye to them and ask the Master for his instructions in the matter of spiritual practices.

Having obtained his instructions, he must then follow them scrupulously, and that alone should constitute his sole devotion. Whatever the Master ordains, that must be taken as Gospel truth, no matter whether it stands the test of mere human reason or not. Our intellect and our reason, after all, are limited and cannot reach the depths to which the Master penetrates. He knows the why and wherefore of his instructions, and like a fully responsible Field Marshal issues his commands.

We must therefore learn to obey him implicitly like a true soldier, and do what he bids. Hafiz, in this context, says:

> *Dye thy prayer carpet in wine if thy Master so desires;*
> *For he is not ignorant of the turns of the highway ahead.*

Mere lip loyalty to the Master never pays. The Master

wants full devotion to what he says, for therein lies the ultimate good of the disciple. In the Gospel it is emphatically declared:

> *If ye love me, keep my commandments.*
>
> JOHN 14:15
>
> *But be ye doers of the Word, and not hearers only, deceiving your own selves.*
>
> JAMES 1:22

Again, mere chatter about spirituality will be of no avail.

> *The scribes and the Pharisees sit in Moses' seat: . . . but do not ye after their works: for they say, and do not.*
>
> MATTHEW 23:2-3
>
> *For the kingdom of God is not in word, but in power.*
>
> I CORINTHIANS 4:20

As the body without the soul is a dead carcass, so talking, if it be alone, is a dead carcass. St. Paul says:

> *Though I speak with the tongues of men and of angels, and have not love, I am become as sounding brass or a tinkling cymbal.*
>
> I CORINTHIANS 13:1

The same may be said of *darshan* or having a look at the Master. It may give you temporary peace and quietness of mind, but the moment you go away the mind begins to run riot again, and reigns supreme over body and soul.

Thus, nothing but doing and performance count on

the Path of the Masters. The Master's words sink deep into the heart; one can hardly think of not following him.

> *If ye abide in me, and my words abide in you, ye shall ask what ye will and it shall be done unto you.*
> *Herein is my Father glorified, that ye bear much fruit; so shall ye be my disciples.*
>
> JOHN 15:7-8

> *Wherefore by their fruits ye shall know them.*
>
> MATTHEW 7:20

> *But he that received seed into the good ground is he that heareth the word, and understandeth it; which also beareth fruit, and bringeth forth, some a hundredfold, some sixty, some thirty.*
>
> MATTHEW 13:23

The world is compared to a harvest (Matthew 13:30) and men at harvest regard nothing but the fruit.

> *Accept the Master's words as Gospel truth, and harvest well the Fruit of Life.*

The words of the Master cannot be detached from the Master. It is from the abundance of the heart that the tongue speaks. The Master is embedded in the Word and his words are expressions of what is in him; that is, Word, Life-impulse, and power. How then can the two be separated from each other? His words undoubtedly pierce through the hearts of the aspirants and none other can know the sweet pangs from which they suffer.

> *As longing for the Lord grew keen, words of the Master pierced my heart; the mind alone knows the pangs; who else can know another's pangs?*

The more one gives weight to the Master's words, the more he grows in grace. True devotion to the Master consists in acceptance of, and doing, what he commands. Guru Ram Das exhorts us that the thought of the Master should ever be a companion, no matter what we may be doing. The Master is hidden in his words, and his words are in fact the real Master.

> *Holy is the Word of the Master, and through It one gets the Elixir of Life; for acceptance of his words gives one immortal life.*
> *Remember ever the Word of the Master, for herein lies real devotion and truth.*
> *Act in conformity to the Master's word; this constiutes contemplation aright.*

The Word of the Master ever abides with the initiates. No power on earth can snatch it away. Fire cannot burn it nor can water sweep it off. It is indestructible and immortal. It fathers the fatherless and protects us at every step. It strikes at the root of all doubt and skepticism. Even the angel of death cannot come near it.

> *Contact Ram Naam through the instructions of the Master;*

> *This nectar can be enjoyed in the company of Saints;*
> *Find thy native home with the help of the Master;*
> *Then there will be no more coming and going.*

One cannot come into the treasure of Naam by the performance of deeds on the plane of the senses.

All persons no doubt sing and hear the Gurbani, but only those benefit from that who really believe in the words of the Master as Gospel truth:

> *Servants and disciples as they come to the Master*
> *Chant the holy verses from scriptures divine;*
> *Chanting and hearing is alone acceptable*
> *From all who with faith accept the words of the Master.*

Persons who time and again meet the Master come to love him more and more; and those who regard his words as Truth become beloved of the Lord.

Whatever the command of the Master may be, it must be followed with unswerving zeal; so that you will be able to take hold of the Shabd, which will lead you back to your native home.

> *Whatever the Master says, that ye must do;*
> *Following the Sound Current, come ye to your own and win for yourself laurels with the help of Naam.*
> *He who acts at the Master's bidding, true comfort is his reward;*

> *By following his behests, O Nanak! one fearlessly crosses over.*

It is absolutely necessary to serve the will of the Master, for in doing so lies the good of the disciple.

Many people indeed meet the Satguru, but that is not enough. For salvation, one has to obey him in thought, word and deed.

> *Everyone looks at the Master, yes, the entire world;*
> *But salvation cannot be had by seeing, without contact with Naam.*

The Master must be an adept in Surat Shabd Yoga and be able to make Shabd manifest within us; that Shabd which does not exist within the nine portals, but is the characteristic of the tenth alone.

When such a Master has been found, it behooves a disciple to wholeheartedly submit himself to his yoke and mold himself accordingly. In doing so, he derives the greatest benefit from his human birth and renders a yeoman's service to his ancestors as well as his descendants, and has nothing of which to be afraid.

> *Blessed indeed is the birth of those who follow the will of the Master;*
> *For they save their families and bring much glory to their mother.*
> *He who molds himself in the way of the Master never gets any ill;*
> *In his way lies the Pool of Nectar and he easily gets to it.*

A disciple who follows the will of the Master gets the Elixir of Life in his own right, and wins the Kingdom of God as his birthright.

> *O man! Follow thou the will of thy Master;*
> *Dwell in thy native home and enjoy life eternal.*

Who understands the will of the Master and follows it scrupulously? One in whom the grace of the Lord works.

> *In whom the Lord's grace works, he alone accepts and follows the Master's words.*

There is no person greater than one who, accepting the words of the Master, realizes God. We must therefore aspire for the Word and try to secure a contact with it through the Sant Satguru.

> *O mind! Always remember the Lord's words;*
> *He who through Word gains his native home*
> *is the crest jewel among men.*

The blessings of Hari Naam are too numerous to be recounted. One who becomes dyed in the color of the Word always chants the glories of God. All his works automatically take the right shape at the right moment.

What he wishes must happen, for Nature herself is at his beck and call. He is freed from all ills and all evils. He loses all thoughts of I-ness and my-ness and never becomes vainglorious.

He rises above the pairs of opposites: riches and poverty, comforts and discomforts, pleasure and pain, fame and obscurity; for he remains in a state serene and with equipoise.

The poison of mind and matter can have no effect on him. While in the world, he is no longer of the world, but is unattached and carefree; he moves about wherever he likes.

The illusions and delusions of the world do not affect him. He escapes the sway of Kal (Time) for time has no bondage for him, nor has space any limitations nor causation any spell.

He gains life everlasting and once again wins back the Kingdom of God, the Garden of Eden from which he was driven because of his first disobedience to God.

He not only saves his own soul but through the power of the Word saves the souls of many others who come in contact with him; yes, the souls of his ancestors and descendants as well.

Blessed indeed is a person who has the good fortune to come into the fold of a Sant Satguru and thus gains the summum bonum of life.

OTHER BOOKS

BY KIRPAL SINGH
> The Crown of Life: A Study in Yoga
> Morning Talks
> Naam or Word
> Prayer: Its Nature and Technique
> A Great Saint—Baba Jaimal Singh: His Life and Teachings
> The Jap Ji: The Message of Guru Nanak
> Spiritual Elixir, Vols. I and II
> The Teachings of Kirpal Singh (compiled by Ruth Seader)
>> Vol. I: The Holy Path
>> Vol. II: Self-Introspection and Meditation
>> Vol. III: The New Life
> Heart to Heart Talks—Vols. I and II (edited by Malcolm Tillis)
> The Night Is a Jungle and Other Discourses of Kirpal Singh
> Man! Know Thyself
> Spirituality: What It Is
> The Mystery of Death
> The Wheel of Life: The Law of Action and Reaction
> Brief Life Sketch of Hazur Baba Sawan Singh Ji Maharaj
> God Power/Christ Power/Guru Power
> Seven Paths to Perfection
> Simran: The Sweet Remembrance of God
> How to Develop Receptivity

BY DARSHAN SINGH
> The Cry of the Soul: Mystic Poetry
> The Secret of Secrets: Spiritual Talks

BY OTHER AUTHORS
> The Beloved Master, edited by Bhadra Sena
> The Saint and His Master, by B.M. Sahai and R.K. Khanna
> Ocean of Grace Divine, edited by Bhadra Sena
> Seeing Is Above All: Sant Darshan Singh's First Indian Tour, edited by H.C. Chadda
> Kirpal Singh: The Story of a Saint, compiled and adapted for children; with illustrations

OTHER BOOKS

Books listed on the preceding page may be ordered through your bookseller or directly from Sawan Kirpal Publications, Route 1, Box 24, Bowling Green, VA 22427; and T.S. Khanna, 8807 Lea Lane, Alexandria, VA 22309.

SAT SANDESH: THE MESSAGE OF THE MASTERS

This monthly magazine is filled with practical and inspiring articles on all aspects of the mystic experience. Discourses by the world's foremost exponent of Surat Shabd Yoga, Sant Darshan Singh, provide the initiate and seeker with invaluable information and guidance on meditation and the spiritual life. Also included are articles by Sant Kirpal Singh and Baba Sawan Singh. Poetry, photos, and other features appear in each issue. For subscription information write: Sat Sandesh, Subscription Dept., Route 1, Box 24, Bowling Green, VA 22427.

SAWAN KIRPAL RUHANI MISSION NEWSLETTER

This bimonthly newsletter contains reports and accounts of Sant Darshan Singh's activities in India, personal experiences of disciples visiting the Master, and satsang news around the world. For free subscription write: Newsletter, Route 1, Box 24, Bowling Green, VA 22427.

FURTHER INFORMATION

Mr. T.S. Khanna, General Representative, 8807 Lea Lane, Alexandria, VA 22309.

Olga Donenberg, Midwest Representative, 6007 N. Sheridan Rd., #14-B, Chicago, IL 60660.

Sunnie Cowen, Southern Representative, 3976 Belle Vista Dr. E., St. Petersburg Beach, FL 33706.

The present living Master, Sant Darshan Singh, resides at Kirpal Ashram, 2 Canal Road, Vijay Nagar, Delhi-110009, India.